Amatus Douw

THE WORLD'S RICHEST ISLANDS OF WEST PAPUA UNDER INTERNATIONAL SYSTEM IN THE 21ST CENTURY

Halaman Moeka

Title   : The World's Richest Islands of West
                   Papua under International System in
                   the 21st Century

Author   : Amatus Douw

Editor   : Nasser Kukkady, DataNZ Limited Auckland,
                   New Zealand
Content Design   : Catur S.
Cover Design   : Bernarda Edoway

Jakarta,   January 2016
ISBN: 978-602-269-153-2

HALAMAN MOEKA PUBLISHING
Jl. Manggis IV No.2 RT 07/04
Tanjung Duren Selatan, Jakarta Barat Telp. (021) 5644157
www.halamanmoeka.net| halamanmoeka@gmail.com

TABLE OF CONTENTS

Table of contents iv
Acronyms & Abreviations vi
Preface & Acknowledgement x
Author Biography xii
Backgrounds xv

Chapter I International Agreements, Foreign Aid & Global World
    Agenda... 1
    I. International Agreements in Practice.................................... 1
        1.1. Two Principal Agreement in the Cold War era 5
        1.2. Bilateral & Multilateral Agreements......................... 11
    II. Foreign Aid Practices 31
        2.1. Multilateral aid 33
        2.2. Official Bilateral Aid 36
        2.3. Unofficial Bilateral Aid... 39
        2.4. Why FA not Delivered to National Liberation
            Movement 40
    III. Global World Agenda 43
        3.1. Democracy & Good Government Development 45
        3.2. Human rights & Humanitarian Development 49
        3.3. Global Security 51
            3.3.1. Armed Conflict Crisis...................................... 53
        3.4. Decolonisation Development.................................... 61
        3.5. MDGs Implication.. 65
    IV. World Global Rule Implication.. 73

Chapter II International Political Actors Interference 81
    I.International Government Attitudes. 81
    II.Regional Government Groups 90
        2.1.Melanesian Spearhead Group.................................... 91
        2.2. Pacific Islands Forum.. 94
        2.3. European Union 99

2.4. African Union & ASEAN 101

III. State Members Attitudes 103

3.1. Netherlands.. 106

3.2. USA & Russia 107

3.3. UK & Vatican State (Rome) 109

3.4. Japan & China 112

3.5. Australia 114

3.6. New Zealand 119

IV.International Non State Actors.................................... 120

4.1. Multinational Corporation Role 120

4.2. Foreign Religions   126

4.3. International Civil Society Groups 131

Chapter III Globalisation Impact **139**

I. Globalisation Discourses 141

1.1. Global Economic Competition.............................. 148

1.2. Global Black Market 153

1.3. Logging & Illegal Logging Impact.......................... 156

1.4. Global Technological Impact 159

II. National & Political Crisis in the Global Era 166

2.1. National Identity 166

2.2. Political Crisis & National Unity 178

III. Economic Globalisation Force 189

Chapter IV Coping Future Development Strategies................... **195**

I. Mobilise Global Assistance.. 195

II. Advocacy to World Body 199

2.1. The 24 Committee of the UN 199

2.2. International Court of Justice 200

2.3. International Criminal Court. 202

III. Nationalism Development 203

3.1. State Nation Formation... 204

3.2. Spiritual Development 207

Bibliography **213**

ACRONYMS AND ABBREVIATIONS

ABC   : Australia Broad Casting
AFC   : Act of Free Choice
APEC   : Asia Pacific Economy Cooperation
ASEAN   : Association of the South East Asian Nations
AUS   : Australia
AusAID   : Australian Aid
BDF   : Bali Democracy Forum
BIN   : Badan Inteligen Negara (State Inteligent Body)
BMP   : Barisan Merah Putih (Red White Line)
BP LNG   : British Petroleum Liquefied Natural Gas
CSOs   : Civil Society Organisations
DAP   : Dewan Adat Papua (Papua Customary Council)
EVI   : Economic Vulnerability Index
FA   : Foreign Aid
FAO   : Food and Agricultural Organisation,
FPPKI   : Forum Perkumpulan Pemuda Kepolisian Indonesia
            (Indonesian Police Youth Association Forum)
FLNKS   : Front de Libération Nationale Kanak et Socialiste
GFG   : Government Force Groups
GKI   : Gereja Kemah Injili (Biblical Evangelical Church)
GKIP   : Gereja Kemah Injili Papua (Papua Evangelical Gospel
            Church)
GKII   : Gereja Kemah Injili Indonesia (Indonesian Gospel
            Evangelical Church)
GIDI   : Gereja Injili Di Indonesia (Gospel Church in Indonesia)
G20   : Groups of 19 states + European Union
G77   : Groups of 77 Developing Nations
HAI   : Human Asset Index
HRL   : Human Rights Law
HRW   : Human Rights Watch
ICC   : International Criminal Court

ICCPR	: International Covenan on Civil and Political Rights
ICESCR	: International Covenant on Economic Social and Cultural Rights
ICG	: International Crisis Groups
ICJ	: International Court of Justice
ICSG	: International Civil Society Groups
ID	: Identity
IFDD	: Indonesia-France Defence Dialogue
IFWP	: International Forum for West Papua
IGO	: International Governmental Organisation
IHRL	: International Human Rights Law
IJPA	: Indonesia-Japan Economic Partnership Agreement
ILO	: International Labour Organisation
ILOAC	: International Law of Armed Conflict
ILWP	: International Lawyer for West Papua
INICB	: Indonesian National Investment Coordination Body
INP	: Indonesian National Police
IODFP	: Indonesian Open Door Foreign Policy
IPE	: International Political Economy
IPWP	: International Parliament for West Papua
JDP	: Jaringan Damai Papua (Papua Peace Network)
KKN	: Korupsi Kolusi Nepotisme (Corruption Collusion Nepotism)
KNPB	: Komite Nasional Papua Barat (West Papua National Committee)
LDCs	: Least Developed Countries
LNG	: Liquefied Natural Gas
LWN	: Lost World Nations
MBFA	: Multilateral and Bilateral Foreign Aid
MDGs	: Millennium Development Goals
MIFEE	: Merauke Integrated Food and Energy Estate
MOU	: Memorandum of Understanding
MNCs	: Multi National Corporations
MSG	: Melanesian Spearhead Groups

MRP	: Majelis Rakyat Papua (Papua People Assembly)
NAFTA	: North America Free Trade Agreement
NATO	: North Atlantic Treaty Organization
NFRPB	: Negara Federal Republik Papua Barat (Republic Federated State of West Papua)
NGOs	: Non-Government Organisations
NKRI	: Negara Kesatuan Republik Indonesia
NLM	: National Liberation Movement
NRN	: Negara Rakyat Nusantara (Islands People State)
NSGT	: Non-Self Governing Territory
NSIG	: Non State Insurgency Groups
NZP	: New Zealand Police
NZ	: New Zealand
ODUS.	: One Door United Service
OECD	: Organisation Economy Cooperation for Development
OUNHCHR	: Office of the United Nations High Commissioner for Human Rights
OPEC	: Organisation Petroleum Export Countries
PCA	: Partnership and Corporation Agreement
PCC	: Pacific Conference of Churches
PDP	: Presidium Dewan Papua (Papua Presidium Council)
PIAG	: Pro-Indonesian Armed Groups
PIF	: Pacific Islands Forum
PNG	: Papua New Guinea
PNWP	: Parliament National for West Papua
PPA	: Papua People Assembly
PPPC	: Public-Private Partnership Centre
PWPIAG	: Pro- West Papuan Independence Armed Groups
RNRTWP	: Rich Natural Resource Territory of West Papua
RSICC	: Rome Statute of the International Criminal Court
SBY	: Susilo Bambang Yudoyono
SPC	: South Pacific Commission
SWOT	: Strenght Weakness Opportunity Treatment
TNI	: Tentara Nasional Indonesia (Indonesian National Army)

TPNPB	: Tentara Pembebasan Nasional Papua Barat (West Papua National Liberation Army)
TV	: Television
UDHR	: Universal Declaration on Human Rights
UK	: United Kingdom
ULMWP	: United Liberation Movement for West Papua
UN	: United Nations
UNAA	: United Nation Association of Australia
UNDC	: United Nations Decolonisation Committee.
UNDP	: United Nation Development Program
UNESCO	: United Nation Educational, Scientific and Cultural Organisation
UNFPA	: United Nation Fund for Population Activities
UNGA	: United Nations General Assembly
UN Habitat	: United Nation Human Settlements
UNHCR	: United Nation High Commissioner for Refugees
UNICEF	: United Nation International Children Emergency Fund
UNRC/UNHC	: United Nation Resident/Humanitarian Coordinator
UNSC	: United Nations Security Council
UNSF	: United Nations Security Force
UNTEA	: United Nation Temporary Executive Administration
UP4B	: Unit Percepatan Pembangunan Papua & Papua Barat (West Papua and Papua Development Acceleration Unit)
USAID	: United State Aid
USIBDD	: United States and Indonesia Bilateral Defence Dialog
WFP	: World Food Program
WHO	: World Health Organisation
WPLM	: West Papua Liberation Movement
WPNA	: West Papua National Authority
WPNCL	: West Papua National Coalition for Liberation
WPNLA	: West Papua National Liberation Army
WPNLM	: West Papua National Liberation Movement
WWF	: World Wide Foundation

PREFACE
AND ACKNOWLEDGEMENT

West Papua is a non-self-governing territory. It not on the Committee of 24, but it was a former NSGT in 1960s. The matters of West Papua are not domestic but are an international issue; the world government and Indonesia cannot undermine the political status and importance of the territory. In the 21st century, the aspiration for West Papuan political independence came under broader attention after the fall of the second Indonesian president, Suharto, in 1998. It was an entry into a new phase under the reformation era of Indonesia. In 2000, West Papua's second congress was held to reform the political landscape and to gain world attraction. West Papuans have gained more confidence to promote and raise global awareness since then. First, the name 'Irian Jaya' was changed to 'Papua' by the fourth Indonesian president, Gusdur, in 2001. Second, a different view of the international community was conceived about West Papua: foreign government has been giving attention to socioeconomic development, some international society groups are giving more attention to NLM to form a state nation, private sectors are concentrating more on investment and trade and some NGOS/CSOs groups are promoting and maintaining human rights laws. Finally, West Papuans are maintaining an optimistic view. They believe they are ready to be a sovereign state. West Papua is undeniably a social minority group in the world, struggling for independent state recognition under international rule.

West Papua is at risk for global political hegemony. West Papuans' struggle to be an independent sovereign state could remain a struggle without international intervention because the political distortion history of some foreign parties has become a key actor.

Third party interaction in this conflicted territory has created multiple impacts. Foreign domination affects all aspects of West Papuan life and is a real danger that could lead to slow genocide. West Papua's aspiration for independence is undercut in the name of a new international order, globalisation, foreign aid and privatisation plus global agendas. All these substantial factors must be considered in modern and global colonisation systems in the 21st century.

I learned some useful knowledge from the university, the some very interesting assignment on international subjects and my direct involvement in international advocacy, sharing, discussion and encouragement, and most importantly people suffering everyday in West Papua, finally those factors made me strong confidence to write a book. The content that I have discussed is definitely a very critical analysis in the interest of education and awareness to the international public audience then readers can come up with good insight and solution strategies in particularly policy makers, world leaders, politicians, human rights defenders, student and underground community wherever they are in our dirty world. Therefore, I praise to the Almighty God (UGATAMEE), Creator and Owner of Universe who given me a good talent and wisdom do this wonderful duty together with my little family in struggling for my beautiful and richest country on the earth.

Firstly, I give a very deeper thanks to my lovely wife; Bernarda Edoway Douw and my son Dounemee Gaitobii Pitoo Douw for their true love every day. Their moral and material support is a very valuable price despite within our simple lifestyle condition.

Secondly, I provide a very special thanks to all of you; My Big Sister Yuliana Douw and her Dougther Alfrida Ukago, Secong Big Sister Marta Douw with your family, last Sister Bendikta Douw and my little Brother Octovianus Douw with your family but also not forget to other relatives.

Thirdly, I also convey many thanks to my wife family: Father in Law (Ruben Edoway), Mother in law (Yustina Badii), Brother in law (Beatus Edoway), Sister in Law (Beatrix Edoway, youngest sister in law; Regina Edoway) including other relatives for your all support in my career.

Fourthly, I give my gratitude for all West Papuan independence fighters both in home and exile for their hard work and contribution for valuable information and their aspiration.

Fifthly, offering a special thanks to my all lectures from Victoria University in Melbourne, Australia who their teaching and encouragement during my study especially, Dr Charless Mafandu, Dr Nicole, Annie Feith and Dr Hellen Hill.

Sixthly, I never forget to say thanks for my friend of 42 West Papuan political asylum for your contribution that we already broken world news about our country. More specific I provide many thanks to my closer friend Florentinus Pirimapun and Paskalis Pisakai for your contribution including Novenus Omabak and Papuana Mote family.

Seventhly, I give my special gratitude for Vanuatu Government and its people for your long standing support, Solomon Islands Government and its people including all Melanesian and Pacific countries and peoples.

Eighthly, my gratitude for all international solidarity groups, they are researcher, journalist, writer, photographer, advocator, parliament member, human activist and lawyer from around the world for their good heart and ongoing support for freedom, justice and peace in West Papua.

Lastly, I am also conveying my special admires to our universe mother despite our human made disaster destroying her body but the earth life never dead.

Author Biography

The author was born in a small village on 10 December 1978 in the Deiyai District in West Papua. He is number 12 of 13 children. He came from a noble family, and he grew up with Mum by Tigi Lake in Duamo Bay, the second biggest lake in the central highland of West Papua. He also lived with his older sister in Enarotali for several years, during which he faced many unfortunate experiences.

First, he was jailed by the Indonesian military for two days with his friends Lukas Degei and Elias Zonggenau when they took firewood from Ugida Mountain during armed war between TNI and TPN OPM, led by the late General Tadius Yogii in 1985. The TNI suspected them of being spies for TPN/OPM. He was only seven years old.

Then, he and his sister were harvesting sweet potatoes from a garden located near the Indonesian army base. He found a piece of human body—a hand—in the garden. The TNI told them they had placed pig meat there for lunch and yelled at them to eat it, laughing.

Because of this persecution, he returned from the Paniai District to his village in Tigi, a long day's walk. The road by passed a large mountain, hills and forests, all full of TNI. Halfway to his destination, he met 25 TNI chatting to OPM/TPN members. They said, 'Hey animal, pig TPN/OPM, where is your General Tadius Yogii'? The boy answered, 'I never know where he is'. They beat him until he bled from his chin. After they let him walk 100 meters, they shot him many times. He continued to his village, where he arrived bleeding.

The author finished junior high school at SMP YPPK Waghete in 1996 and senior high school at SMA Gabungan in 2000. He wanted to become an Air Force pilot to fight back against the Indonesian army, but when he did not qualify because of his height, he discontinued the pursuit. He studied at the State University of Papua in Manokwari for four years, but he never completed his study due to his involvement in the Independence Movement. Finally, he left university and escaped to Australia in 2006 as a political asylum-seeker.

He began his new life in a new country. He first learned English and continued to study until he graduated with a Bachelor of Arts in International Community Development at Victoria University in Melbourne, Australia. He never stopped advocating for West Papuan independence during his study period. His third year of student placement was the most rewarding. The Pacific Islands Forum of 2011 in Auckland attracted the key United Nations leader Ban Ki-moon, who discussed the West Papuan right of self-determination.

The author was also actively involved in the West Papua National Coalition for Liberation, lobbying for Melanesian countries until 2013, when he married Bernarda Edoway, a West Papuan woman who graduated a Master of regional government administration. Together, they applied to become members of the Melanesian Spearhead Group. His wife was the only women who played important role in the application submission to the MSG Secretariat table. He was a West Papuan leader, founding a West Papuan umbrella group of the United Liberation Movement for West Papua in 2014. He is a West Papuan ambassador of the United Liberation Movement for West Papua for Australia and Pacific countries. He actively lobbies and advocates for the self-determination of West Papua.

BACKGROUND

West Papua Territory is located at the central border between the Pacific and Asia region, only 300 km north of Northern Territory in Australia. West Papua is the western half of the whole New Guinea Islands; the eastern half is the independent state of Papua New Guinea. The different names of the islands were given by westerners when they voyaged into this region in the 15th-18th centuries until Indonesian era today.

West Papua has changed its name several times in the colonial history: West New Guinea, West Netherland New Guinea, West Irian, Irian Jaya and Papua. Nowadays, with Indonesian rule, this territory is divided into two Indonesian provinces, West Papua and Papua. However, native people called West Papua for their stand for political independence, then in this book writer would like to use West Papua, the more common name.

West Papua's political status is an unrecoverable matter even in the 21st century. Historically, this territory was a former Dutch Colony in 1828-1962. West Papua proclaimed its independence on 1st of December 1961. Due to Cold War pressure, Indonesia took over West Papua from the hand of UNTEA illegally under US mediated *New York Agreement* signed on 15 August 1962. This agreement should be called a secret Cold War agreement, as the West Papuans themselves were never involved only Indonesia and the Netherlands were signatory parties. US hegemony in the Asia Pacific regions was a victory to gain Asia Pacific power.

In the New York Agreement it was agreed to hold a referendum called Act of Free Choice. Act of Free Choice implementation totally violated the international principle of one man one vote. Indonesia not only ignored international rule but also a fundamental West Papuan political principle, *one people one soul*. Only1025 people were asked, and these were handpicked to vote for integration into Indonesia under their military controlled consultation system.

54 years of Indonesian colonization for this Melanesian territory resulted in more than 600,000 Papuans being killed. Systematic genocide programs were very cleverly designed by Indonesia to threaten the West Papuan people. These programs included sustainable military operation zone and transmigration system, Indonesian nationalism education, Asian culture teaching undergone by close door foreign policy of second Indonesian president, Suharto for 32 years of dictatorship regime until 1998. Indonesian open door foreign policy begun since a massive demonstration by civil society groups across Indonesian region even this reformation also backed by world community tension.

In 2001 a special autonomy law was offered to West Papua. The West Papuan people rejected this law, asking for an internationally mediated dialogue and a new referendum toward independence. This resulted in many West Papuan leaders being killed. The failure of special autonomy rule implementation became a target for international public criticism. Four European countries visited West Papua and found that the reality was there was no improvement as a whole. The US, Australia, New Zealand and the UK urged Indonesia to open a dialogue, but they never responded. SBY prepared another plan, the UP4B, which the West Papuan people rejected. The former vice president travelled around the world to convince the foreign government that the new policy had failed. Another policy was born: special autonomy plus. All foreign aid went to support the failed special autonomy, but there was no significant social or economic development: in 2014 there is 80% of the population fell under the poverty line, and HIV, AIDS, human rights violations, marginalisation, extrajudicial murder and jailing were all rooted to the ground. The West Papuan people only want a referendum and recognition of independence by state nation, but a small number of people support the Indonesian rule of special autonomy.

The Indonesian president, Joko Widodo, promised to have a genuine dialogue to settle the problems in West Papua. In 2015, the independence movement and rights to self-determination was recognised by Melanesian Spearhead Group's state members, who obtained observer status, and Pacific Islands Forum agreed to conduct a fact-finding mission.

Profile

Name of Territory: West Papua

Flag: Morning Star

National Anthem: Hay, My Land of Papua

Administering Power: Netherland

Occupying Power: Indonesia

Internationally Legitimated Political Party: United Liberation Movement for West Papua

Population: 1.7 Million Natives & 2 Million migrants

Currency: Rupiah

Religion: 95 % Christian, 1% Muslim, 0% Buddhist plus Hindu and 4%Native Papuan Religion (Bunani, Koreri, etc.)

Chapter I

INTERNATIONAL AGREEMENTS, FOREIGN AID AND GLOBAL WORLD AGENDA

I. INTERNATIONAL AGREEMENTS IN PRACTICE

West Papua is not a signatory party for all kinds of international agreements but the only non-state party, which has obligated to uphold the rule of law of these fundamental treaties. To maintain international law, West Papua has to choose liberation from any colonialist hand and form an independent sovereign nation state; it's definitely the best option and solution. Therefore, the following international mandatory agreements are essential legal instruments that ensure to reclaim the West Papuan political sovereignty:

- International Resolution of 1514 and 1541; *granting independence for colonial people and territory* signed on 14 December 1960 by state members. This fundamental resolution is part of the implementation on the inalienable rights to self-determination and undeniably guarantees all national liberation movement activities around the world, in order to regain their political sovereign rights if the territory was formerly or under colonial rule.

- UDHR signed on 10 December 1945 by state members. This human rights law ensures people and territories who struggle for their external and internal rights of self-determination, both indigenous people and non-self-governing territory who lay a claim for their independent nation state.

- UN charter, treaties and covenant including two legally binding international agreements on ICESCR plus ICCPR. In this regard, their social economic development, cultural survival and political development including freedom of movement, speech and association are protected by obligatory state.

The above international principal laws need globally applicable lawful tools for colonised people and territories not just rhetorical theory due to its principle world mandate and moral duty, hence colonialist states, particularly Indonesia and Netherlands must pay in order to sustain their main obligation by giving recognition to West Papuan demands for their independence sovereignty rights.

West Papua was a part of non-self-governing territory on the decolonisation list that is obligated by international law to maintain the rule of law and committed to monitor its realisation. After removal of its decolonisation status from the UN, West Papuans nationalists first formed WPNLM in order to actively play a role in international political flora. WPNLM as non-state actor requires upholding world political norms and ethics, normally as political actor keenly monitoring and endorsing state members' duty on international law enforcement in delivering international conflict resolution treaties. In the realization of the international resolution 1514 and 1541, historically triple colonialist nations Netherlands, Indonesia and United State of America had violated the production of the two political arrangements of *New York and Rome* on the future West Papua territorial status quo in the year of 1962. In the final result of the comprehension, both the agreements had produced an international ratification of the resolution 2504 under UN authority; their practise was absolutely in denial of the inalienable rights for self-determination. Even in the realization aspect for the UDHR were ignored on the whole for many years, hence, on one side West Papuan independence struggle is correcting and remaining all state stakeholder, then they will be able to show their capacity, how important and crucial in accomplishment of its rule of law, who were their contracted parties and most influential states players.

Indonesia is constantly very sceptical on the international arrangement both non-binding and binding protocols in some fundamental affairs. Why Indonesia is usually never a signatory state, some reasonable point of views are, avoiding from public accountability, world obligation and responsibility otherwise facing a serious sanction and being brought to the world court, if Indonesia violates on these obligation. On the other hand, Indonesia has always been cleverer to minimise the issue of West Papua by IODFP, by just allowing its foreign partners who are committed to defend what Indonesia stands for, it completely disobeys these world treaties in order to provide the better security, democracy and welfare for their population without discriminatory action. Most essentially, these international treaties are eligible and applicable in conformity with the factual situation in Indonesia if the related world organisations are necessary to monitor its achievement. On the contrary, Indonesia just ratified six treaties and signed 4 treaties in 2012; in October 2005 before *or* after 5 years in the 21st century, the UNDP's report stated, *the Indonesian House of Representatives ratified two long-awaited UN covenants, namely the UN Covenant on Civil and Political Rights and the Covenant on Economic Social and Cultural Rights.* These six treaties are not sufficient to fix the complex matters; Indonesia is the fourth biggest populated nation, with many violations and war, which are needed to be resolved with third party supervision.

In 2006, Indonesia became a member of UN human rights council, since then many countries and world communities are doing some regular monitoring for its human rights record particularly in connection with West Papuan affairs. One of the most eligible treaties under the UPR that Indonesia was suggested to sign is the RSICC due to the ongoing slow armed war between Indonesian state forces and WPNLA in the very long time, both the party more often announce their open war, which were debated widely since world community gives no reaction. Below is an example of how Indonesia shuns from international treaties unlike Philippines.

Table 1. Signatory States on Important International Treaties

International Treaties signed by Indonesia and its Neighbouring States

Information sourced from Amnesty International Report 2012

Legend:
- ● State is party
- ○ Signed but not yet ratified

State	International Convent on Civil and Political Rights (ICCPR)	(first) Optional protocol to the ICCPR	Second Optional Protocol to the ICCPR, aiming at the abolition of the death penalty	Optional Protocol to the ICESCR (not in force)	International Covenant on Economic, Social and Cultural Rights (ICESCR)	Convention of the Elimination of All forms of Discrimination against Women (CEDAW)	Optional Protocol to CEDAW	Convention on the Rights of Children (CRC)	Optional Protocol to the involvement of Children in armed conflict	International Convention on the Elimination of All Forms of Racial Discrimination	Convention against torture and Other cruel, Inhuman or Degrading Treatment or Punishment	Optional Protocol to the convention against Torture	International convention for the Protection of All Persons from Enforced Disappearance	Convention relating to the Status of Refugees (1951)	Protocol relating to the status of Refugees (1967)	Convention on the Reduction of Statelessness (1954)	Convention on the Reduction of Statelessness (1961)	International Convention on the Protection of the Rights of All Migrant Workers and Members of Their Families	Rome Statute of The International Criminal Court
Australia	●	●	●	●		●	●	●	●	●	●	●	○	○	●	●	●		●
Indonesia	●			●		●	○	●	○	●	●		○					○	
Malaysia								●		●									
New Zealand	●	●	●	●		●	●	●	●	●	●	●		●	●		●		●
Papua New Guinea	●		●			●		●		●				●	●				
Philippines	●	●	●	●		●	●	●	●	●	●	●		●	●	●		●	●
Singapore								●		●	●								
Solomon Islands			●	○		●	○	●	○	●				●	●				○
Timor-Leste	●		●	●	○	●	●	●	●	●	●		○	●	●			●	●

I.1. TWO PRINCIPAL AGREEMENT IN THE COLD WAR ERA

Without West Papuan participation, two crucial arrangements were signed, *New York Agreement and Rome Agreement, it is best called as two secret cold war agreements.* These two secret cold war agreements made were aimed to rule up a future destiny on territorial status quo and economic development for West Papuan. In the process both the agreements were manoeuvred by colonialists in which West Papuan people were not party on that furtive arrangement. Unfortunately it totally disobeyed the international legal rule and norms. US mediated a New York Agreement between Dutch and Indonesia, signed on 15 August 1962, after three weeks' time US Ambassador to Indonesia, Mr Elsworth Bunker proposed another new accord of three party agreement called *Rome Agreement* which were signed by triple party amongst Indonesia, Netherland Kingdom and USA in the capital city of Italy on 30th September 1962. Public critics raised objections as to why two agreements were taken in a month; the content was controversial in their accomplishment of both the awful agreement; rational questions were asked as to why the Rome agreement was made in Italy not in Netherlands, Indonesia, USA, or West Papua. Many people assumed that secret party was involved, whether this agreement was truly approved by Pope on behalf of Vatican government or not. From the critical question and analysis, we come to the conclusion that it was a true manipulation in *realpolitik*, neglecting the rule of law, international norms and the code of conducts. Both the agreements were made during cold war era, so the colonialist groups mind might be full of freeze. Nonetheless when the right time comes this secret cold war agreement will be examine in the right of world justice table.

Given below are original copy of the New York Agreement and the Rome Agreement.

(a) New York Agreement:

On 15 August 1962, the negotiation between Indonesia and Dutch conducted at Headquarter UN in New York. In the negotiation, Indonesia represented by Soebandrio and Dutch represent by Jan Herman van Roijenand C.W.A. Schurmann. Content of the New York Agreement are:

a. *Dutch will transfer West Papuan Territory to the UNTEA who established by UN Secretary General.*

b. *UN flag will rising during transition period.*

c. *Raising Indonesian flag and Dutch flag will be arrange by agreement between UN and each of both Government.*

d. *UNTEA will assist West Papuan Police in maintain security. Indonesia soldier and Dutch Soldier under General Secretary Authority in the transition period.*

e. *Indonesia, by UN assistance will giving opportunity for people in West Papua to taking decision freely through (1) Consultation with West Papuan People (2) arrangement for act of free choice Timetable (3) question formulation in act of choice about West Papuan want for (a) joint into Indonesia (b) self-independence, (4) equal rights adult, men and women to take part in act of free choice will held accordance to international standards. The act of free choice will be held before end of 1969.*

(b). The Rome Agreement provided among other this the following:

1. *Referendum or the Act of Free Choice set for 1969 in the New York Agreement of August, 1962. To be delayed or possible cancelled.*

2. *Indonesia to rule West Papua for the next twenty - five years (25) effective from the first of May, 1963.*

3. *Method to be use in implementation of the Act of Free Choice or Referendum would be "musyawarah system" in accordance with the Indonesian Parliamentary practice.*

4. *UN's final report on the implementation of the Act of Free Choice presented to the UN General Assembly is accepted without open debate.*

5. *The United State of America is responsible to make an investment through Indonesian State Companies for the Exploration of mineral, petroleum and other resources of West Papua.*

6. *The USA guarantees the Asian Development Bank US $. 30 Million To be granted to the United Nation Development Programme (UNDP) to develop West Papua for a Period of twenty-five (25) years.*

7. *The USA guarantees the World Bank funds for Indonesia to plan and implement its transmigration program where Indonesian was resettled in West Papua starting from 1977.*

The New York Agreement was totally manipulated by Rome Agreement in the content and its implementation. It had been found to be extremely controversial in realisation and none of them truly guarantee the rights of self-determination exercise for West Papuan people by proper referendum mechanism.

An historical question raised up by many people was that, why UN and U.S negotiated with three of the most European prominent leaders namely Pope and two European Queens, Elisabeth II and Juliana in the process of transferring the territory. This assumption was vital to know why these three world leaders agreed to transfer the territory from the hand of UNTEA to the unitary state of Indonesia, surely indicating their absolute regret dealt beyond. Ironically what the Pope approved was truly immoral and sinful action against His stand for salvation and peace. Their western hegemony interests of Christianity and capitalist expansion against the communist & socialist power was presented into former Dutch New Guinea Territory and Indonesia. Rome agreement became a critical point; there was no political change after 25 years of term. As a form of protest and the realisation for the key point of Rome Agreement, a new independence declaration led by Dr Thomas Wainggai on 14 December 1988 was made at Mandala Stadium, Jayapura capital city of Papua province now. There was no reaction by the Pope or Vatican when the Indonesian army charged Thomas with lifetime imprisonment in an Indonesian prison and many of his friends jailed for more than 10 years. For decades, Vatican president Pope's attention was totally negligent in restoring this Rome agreement which was a failure for humanitarian salvation mission and also to protect and create a freedom for his 48 % of West Papuan Catholic followers.

The New York Agreement has stirred the Rome Agreement; due to this change some principal point of New York Agreement has extraordinarily caused some fundamental constraint. Those restrictions were international referendum standards manipulated to domestics or colonialist referendum scheme "Consultation", UN report of the result without public debate, transmigration plan target to Asian migrant escalation, Indonesia and Netherland guarantee for exploitation of natural resource in West Papua. The worth of 30 Million US dollars through ADB was granted to UNDP for 25 years era versus 25 years Military Zone in the territory, resulting in 100.000 Papuan deaths, UNDP did not operate their agreed term because in 1966 Indonesia withdrew from UN member. US empowered through World Bank to which the money trained Indonesian civilian armed groups support a transmigration plan, which had already impacted unending horizontal conflict between migrant community and native Papuan people. Indonesian migrant population has been increasing almost 10 folds, equally native West Papuan has been decreasing

10 folds according to demographic measurement; mortality rate was high for West Papuan, thus migration domination was stronger and their population growth was vast because of lower mortality rate. Social welfare development program by ADB in which UNGA mandated to Indonesia was a failure in the last 25 years, the UNDP has strictly dictated by the national authority of Indonesia in many-many years, this UN development agency was unable to present it so if UNDP made report it might be misinformation or weaker because of dysfunction.

Final result of the illegal Rome and New York Agreement had born international resolution of 2504 in the session of 1813, the UN plenary meeting in1969. Given below is the original copy:

2504 (XXIV): Agreement between the Republic of Indonesia and the Kingdom of the Netherlands concerning West New Guinea (West Irian)

The General Assembly,

Recalling its resolution 1752 (XVII) of 21 September 1962, in which it took note of the Agreement of 15 August 1962 between the Republic of Indonesia and the Kingdom of the Netherlands concerning West New Guinea (West Irian). Acknowledged the role conferred upon the Secretary-General in the Agreement and authorized him to carry out the tasks entrusted to him therein,

Recalling also its decision of 6 November 1963 to take note of the report of the Secretary-General on the completion of the United Nations Temporary Executive Authority in West Irian,

Recalling further that the arrangements for the act of free choice were the responsibility of Indonesia with the advice, assistance and participation of a special representative of the Secretary-General, as stipulated in the Agreement,

Having received the report on the conduct and results of the act of free choice submitted by the Secretary-General in accordance with article XXI, paragraph 1, of the Agreement,

Bearing in mind that, in accordance with article XXI, paragraph 2, both parties to the Agreement have recognized these results and abide by them,

Noting that the Government of Indonesia, in implementing its national development plan, is giving special attention to the progress of West Irian, bearing in mind the specific conditions of its population, and that the Government of the Netherlands, in close cooperation with the Government of Indonesia, will continue to render financial assistance for this purpose, in particular through the Asian Development Bank and the institutions of the United Nations,

1. *Takes note of the report of the Secretary-General and acknowledges with appreciation the fulfilment by the Secretary-General and his representatives of the tasks entrusted to them under the Agreement of 15 August 1962 between the Republic of Indonesia and the Kingdom of the Netherlands concerning West New Guinea (West Irian);*

2. *Appreciates any assistance provided through the Asian Development Bank, through institutions of the United Nations or through other means to the Government of Indonesia in its efforts to promote the economic and social development of West Irian.*

Another multilateral arrangement was Canberra Agreement signed by five European colonialists namely Netherlands, France, British, Australia, New Zealand plus United States on the political status for the pacific territories. West Papua was included on the colonial territories in the Pacific Rim, this agreement aimed to facilitate full independence attainment for the Pacific Islands colonial territories under the regional block of South Pacific Commission formed in 1946. West Papua was part of the SPC founding member under the Dutch rule; Markus Youwe and Markus Wonggor Kaisepo in the name of West Papuan representative have ever participated in the severe meeting. Fortunately, some European colonised pacific territories attained their full independence sovereignty state such as Vanuatu from British and France, PNG from Australia, Fiji under England, Solomon Island from British and other as well. By global force and regionalism interest the SPC was moved to Pacific Island Forum for broader context. The implementation on their Canberra agreement has completely ignored to enhance West Papua's inalienable rights and their regional identity, based on this Canberra agreement should be restored again in order to maintain regional identity. West Papuan continuingly seeks an membership status at PIF in many ways to achieve political goal, as umbrella political organisation of West Papuan, the ULMWP have plans to apply a Forum Observer in 2015-2016 to retain back their past membership status quo. So if West Papuan as member fully participates in the PIF, it will ensure the Canberra Agreement without misjudgement on it by Indonesia and Netherlands.

I.2. BILATERAL AND MULTILATERAL AGREEMENTS

After illegal UN resolution of 2405 was ratified by the signatory states, confidently Indonesia made on the ranges of the multilateral and bilateral agreements with international and regional governmental organizations including individual countries in dealing to West Papuan's Affairs. The 84 state members who signed the illegal resolution of 2405 exactly manipulated by their bilateral and multilateral arrangement with Indonesia on behalf of West Papua's sensitive and rich natural resources territory. Conversely, the other 30 absent nations or no signatory nations of the 2405 resolution have not dealt their bilateral ties agreement with Indonesia, sometime those nations have seen their good response on public debate at

UN when Vanuatu spoke up on West Papuan inalienable rights and independence.

Indonesia is happy, free and active for seeking and offering whatever cooperation wants it to, whether investment and partnership with foreign government. The above 84 nations are their first target on the benefit of defending Indonesian sovereignty and integrity on West Papua territory likewise Indonesia is first target of the 84 nations. Indonesian open door foreign policy (IODFP) is considered unquestionably to be core instrument for trade and investment interest, as by this way it capably creates space for global competitor accessibility into West Papua. Their negative ambiguity will always defy their world obligation for any good political initiative in the practise for example eradication on the world colonialism in which Indonesia became host country for UN Decolonisation meeting several times in the 21st century excluded West Papua's political status to be addressed. Majority vote at the 24 committee comes from the 84 state members, consequently, less vote to reinscribe West Papua territory to decolonisation desk.

Indonesia very likely has been building partnership with newly formed independent state nations from the Middle East, Asian, African, Pacific, American Latin and Caribbean region in order to block off their support for decolonisation process over West Papua when it rises again into regional and international forum flora. Indonesia has a strong historical sentiment to Israel and others, Indonesia as main backers for Palestine independence, nonetheless, different case to South Africa has good link since Indonesia joined G20 for their joint investment venture in West Papua. These 84 nations sustain the resolution 2405 by many ways, bilateral and multilateral cooperation mostly in multiple sectors, Indonesia back in their domestic matters. Some of the case studies are:

A. BILATERAL AGREEMENTS

Indonesia made bilateral agreement with five veto nations or five permanent seats at UNSC and other powerful countries around the world in the 21st century. The content in their cooperation agreement more defensively protect Indonesian sovereignty on domestic political affairs or meddles *non-intervention* and investment protection. However, their bilateral agreement undeniably has a negative impact on the life quality for the native people in the slow armed conflict region of West Papua. It provides some examples of their bilateral agreements on strategic aspect such as defence and security, trade and investment, environment and human rights.

1. Indonesia-US bilateral agreement is very unique towards West Papua. Their 21st century bilateral agreement in defence and security is undeniably motivated by political, economic and security power competition in the modern time. Their military ties was cut off due to the killing incident of two US citizens in Timika 2002, but was reactivated again for continuing military training in 2005 after three years. Indonesia-USA comprehensive partnership in military training was developed in 9 May 2010 when Barack Obama first visited Indonesia. Both the head of States discussed their effective action in 2010 and 2011.United States and Indonesia Bilateral Defence Dialog (USIBDD) agreed to annual defence dialogue. Indonesia's first biggest donor for military equipment, training and finance is the USA. Indonesia feels very proud as Obama had his childhood, almost 8 years in Indonesia with his Indonesian step Father, Obama considers Indonesia as his second home country. Sadly West Papuan had very high emotional pressure on him being half black, they opposed him. West Papuan confronted him by having peaceful rally against their bilateral agreement on defence and investment during his visit. During Bali democracy meeting, Hillary Clinton advised that open dialogue is important to resolve ongoing human rights violation and political unrest

as ethical approach to uphold international pacific settlement. Nevertheless, US should have a closer engagement with Indonesia in order to reach new bilateral agreement on peaceful approach on West Papua or by any other means they should restore their past mistake which had failed to implement their *New York Agreement*.

USA and Indonesia met in 2015 October; President Jokowi offered a new agreement to President Obama in relation to greedy ambition to the Transnational Pacific Partnership for trade. When looking at the West Papua border line region between Asia and Pacific, it potentially gives a real impact for trade interest for these nations who have joined under the TPP treaty. Indonesia is an open economy as Jokowi said to his counterpart, meanwhile Obama criticised the continuing of Indonesian military operation in West Papua, Obama's reaction was very good according to media language. However, there was no further preventive effort taken by Obama to reduce this armed conflict, which kills native Papuans everyday which creates awareness in the international community about the US-Indonesia military ties. Two former presidents of both countries, W Bush and SBY's administration was the beginning of the military operation history in the 21st century.

2. Indonesia and Russian bilateral relations began in 1950s. In 2003 they made an agreement called *Declaration of the Republic of Indonesia and the Russian Federation on the Framework of Friendly and Partnership Relations in the 21st Century*. SBY visited Russia to make a new military and defence cooperation, which was signed by two head of states were SBY and Putin in 2006 in their agreement. Russia granted $US 1 billion for procurement of Russian Military Equipment for 5 years extension. Joint statement made by both states on 7 September 2007 agreed to have a closer relationship for peace and security in Asia and Pacific conflict, supporting the international resolution through UNSC and UNGA on Arab-Israel conflict in helping Palestine independence initiative. With their

bilateral ties, they are not only concerned about West Papua's long enduring conflict, but also how they can use their government for global security and peace. They also give their support to the Iran's nuclear program to be accepted by IAEA. They have also endorsed to Kosovo peace dialogue. Russia endorsed to establish Nuclear Industry in Biak Island in West Papua. Not minding the Jakarta –Papua's peaceful dialogue; they close off to look at their home affairs which are to be internationalised or to make it into an international agenda.

3. Indonesia-UK defence and trade agreements are dependable on each other. The bilateral agreement was signed in the past and is now reindorsed under Indonesia-EU partnership agreement after 21 century. Through their past military cooperation, British army were involved in killing over hundreds of West Papuan in Timika when the OPM fighter broke Freeport Mine pipe line in 1996. It had bhrougt a real negative impact as it not only took many lives but also many lost their materials. President SBY and PM Tony Blair made UK-Indonesia partnership forum in Bali for modern and dynamic partnership at all aspect, BP LNG started to operations in West Papua province after Indonesia and British signed bilateral cooperation for investment in 2006. In 2014, SBY was called for UK owned Churchill mining to the international criminal court for claiming over 2 billion royalty fund. SBY never mentioned about royalty and compensation from the BP LNG for West Papuan even after his bilateral meeting with British Prime Minister and Queen Elisabeth. Queen Elisabeth grants special gift SBY for the Gold, the Gold came from Freeport McMoran along with Rio Tinto which shared 40% of it. Indonesia and UK relationship would be suitable to call bilateral ties for gold. Bilateral meeting between new Indonesian Foreign Minister and UK Foreign Minister had also agreed to have investment and trade in 2015 in which UK has five major investor countries in Indonesia.

4. Indonesia-China bilateral agreement has been renewed. Indonesia does not lose the Asian nation with veto rights at UN. China is the second biggest investor country in Indonesia; hence both the countries have introduced more defensive investment security agreement. Indonesia-China bilateral trade agreement was signed on 2 October 2013, both the president have agreed to increase 8 billion by 2015. In their meeting they also agreed to increase defence and military cooperation, three reasons in relation to the West Papua, firstly to counter US navy, otherwise to provide military aid for West Papua, secondly is to secure their investment and thirdly Indonesia's secret initiative is to influence China get Melanesian states stand on Indonesian side when the West Papuan independence voice rises up at regional forum of MSG and PIF.

5. Indonesia-France Cooperation. Indonesia made bilateral ties with second European veto rights nation at UNSC, which are important in relevance to the security and political agenda. Their bilateral agreement made in 2011 in three strategic aspects is military, energy and tourism. They set an Indonesia-France Defence Dialogue (IFDD) in response to international armed conflict. France appreciated Indonesian stand on Ukrainian matter for bringing Middle East peace. In foreign ministerial meeting on August 2013 Foreign Minister of France, Laurent Fabius promised France Military Companies will back up Indonesian weaponry modernisation, which even made its construction. It will be really challenging to look at back yard, domestic non-internationalised armed conflict between TNI and TPN excluding of their agreement. Now Indonesia uses modern weapon in their military operation against independence fighters in West Papua, France government unwisely enforces its military aid to Indonesia despite that the European Union Parliament has banned military aid to Indonesia.

6. Indonesia-Australia Bilateral Treaty. Their strong relationship had built when West Papua's affairs go to the world community's attention including their citizen who has given more pressure on Indonesian and Australian government in the early of the 21 century. The Lombok Treaty was signed in 2006 by Australia and Indonesia to counter separatist movement and border control as part of outcome of the 43 political asylum seeker who landed in Australia by traditional boat in same year. Their political motivation beyond its cooperation violated the international norms, because firstly without invitation by key interested party of Papuan groups for seeking a peaceful resolution; secondly definitely their corporation does not recognises the foreign aid plan for better security and safety; Thirdly they denied the principles of international treaties such as freedom of want, freedom of movement, freedom of association and freedom of participation.

Other agreement came along in 2012 for defence cooperation; this proposes to train Indonesia military in Australia and is aimed to counter terrorist but in the reality for killing native West Papuan. Their misarrangement in defence and security, investment and business are very dominant, under their cooperation exploiting out rich natural resources and protecting their company operating in West Papua will be taken care of. Transnational crime treaty is also part of their bilateral benefit, the deal has nothing to protect regional stability and security, there are many smuggling people coming from Indonesia, apart from this even illegal emigrant and illegal fishing takes place. West Papua territory is the border line between Australia and Indonesia from the Southern side, anything with their interests always has an impact on West Papua. That is why it is crucial to examine the territorial status of West Papua land both politically and legally through international mechanism. Australia does not need to think about investment in Indonesia, but morally more urgent is human security and human rights,

Australia will have high risks when trying to control smuggling and boat people, if West Papua is still part of Indonesia. Australia already is a Muslim targeted country to take over and many terrorist networks will come this way.

7. Indonesia-Japan Bilateral Arrangement. Indonesia-Japan signed a bilateral cooperation between President Indonesia SBY and Prime Minister of Japan called as the Indonesia-Japan Economic Partnership Agreement (IJPA), which was formed in 2008 by joint agreement between their foreign ministers. According to this agreement Japan ensured good democracy, human security and peace building financial aid agreement goes through that channel. In this agreement they had also renewed their six past agreements in term of provincial level, one of them was Irian Jaya (now West Papua) Yamagata Prefecture. Irian Jaya-Yamagata prefecture arrangement on investment cooperation between Indonesia and Japan who are strategically placed to establish their economic business in West Papua territory. In 2000 Japan had dominated in national automotive market, it has seen too monopolistic character in the domestic market system. West Papuan people bought Japanese car, these were low quality car only three months after which it was broken, economically also from an considerable aspect. Indonesian government provide money for few number of Papuan who spying West Papuan independence activities then politically also at risk because West Papuan is in very poor condition.

Japan critically persisted Indonesia to ensure human security and human rights development during several international forum. Japan has a historical link with West Papua and Indonesia in the cold war era, to maintain that relationship; they have opened new phase relationship by elaborating into a current global issue that directly affects West Papua. Their human security and democracy arrangement was not successful in order to bring a real change on those domestic barriers and conflicts. Japan is funding peace aid to Jakarta authority does not allow to grant those national peace network groups. JDP in itself has been promoting a Jakarta-Papua peace dialogue in the name of Land of peace project based in conflict Indonesian province in Jayapura. Other non-private institution both in Jakarta and Papua should get enough funding like LIPI who besides JDP work to promote a peace roadmap in settling the long enduring conflict between West Papuan and Indonesia.

8. Indonesia-New Zealand Bilateral affairs. Second developed nation in the pacific after Australia is very potential nation for Indonesia. Indonesia and New Zealand defence and security bilateral agreement was signed on 7 January 2011. This arrangement was made in their cooperation towards preventing and combating transnational crimes between New Zealand Police (NZP) and the Indonesian National Police (INP). Bilateral defence cooperation resumed in 2006 for military activities in training and cooperation in humanitarian operational and regional forum. In 2014 trained 1000 INP in Papua province provided the course for effective community policing and transnational crime course collaborated with Victoria University 2013 and was attended by INP officials. In 2014, after NZ trained Indonesian national police have been involved in killing West Papuan, the government of New Zealand remained to cut off defence and security ties. However, on 3 March 2015, both foreign ministers signed their cooperation agreement on security and defence. New Zealand continuing to train Indonesian National Police for their bilateral interest. New Zealand will not change Indonesian police repressive behaviour; more empower to do persecution of their pacific native people in the land of pacific territory of West Papua.

9. Indonesia-Norway Bilateral Agreement. An agreement was bilaterally made between Indonesia and Norway in Oslo 2014.

Indonesian President SBY and Norway's Prime Minister Stoltenberg signed their bilateral agreement on reducing deforestation in which Indonesia has obligation to reduce 26% gas emission by 2020. Rainforest foundation Norway criticises why 1.6 million hectare MIFEE in West Papua region, which SBY had launched in 2010 January. Indonesian environmental organisations stated that the MIFEE project will bring huge number of workers leading to disastrous transmigration programme. Even more importantly local community was not involved in the meeting for Environmental Assessment Impact conducted on 13 February 2014 at muting district. Norway government should be constantly monitored and needed to enhance the partnership with environmental and educational institution including community organisation for more accurate information and investigation of those environmental and human rights related matters.

10. Indonesia-Germany Bilateral Affairs. In October 2009 bilateral meeting held in Germany between SBY and Counsellor Angela Merkel discussed their cooperation, a year later both the states made an agreement in 2010 on technical and financial cooperation. Germany addressed a regional autonomy in a good government in the bilateral agreement because Germany is one of biggest donator for special autonomy development fund to Indonesia in relation of the current status of two provinces in West Papua territory. It was not only with government, Indonesia and private sector (MNC) agreement also had passed on Monday 4 March 2013 in Berlin. Klause Leske and Indonesian industrial minister, Panggah Susanto also agreed their private investment commitment in construction chemist industry that produce methanol and propenol by total investment US$ 2 million will start in 2019 in Bintuni Bay, West Papua.

Knowing Germany to be as the world's first higher technology state, Indonesia was not wrong to embrace Germany; it bilaterally was an enormous deal in terms of technological industry development in the geographical risky regions like West Papua within Indonesia. But Germany needs to know what West Papuan needs today and Indonesian has bad reputation on using foreign aid, infrastructure development in region like this definitely not workable due to many challenges under the colonial administration of Indonesia. West Papuan wants Germany's foreign aid and technological investment, even transfer of technology after the independence come through for the Papuans if Germany has good willingness to assist West Papuan.

11. Indonesia-Netherlands bilateral relationship: Historically, Indonesia and West Papua were former colony of the Netherland Kingdom. After Dutch recognised independence of Indonesia and West Papua became integral part of Indonesia illegally, their Bilateral Cooperation begun into a new phase. Indonesia-Netherland Bilateral Agreement morally is of higher degree in terms of maintaining world obligation for inalienable rights, independence and decolonisation. Their development cooperation, political, trade and investment were reached after 2005 since Ben Bot made a public statement upon political and moral endorsement during Indonesian independence commemoration day on 17 August 2005.

Now their relationship has built up more defensive and strong in the political matter, investment and trade. Former President of Indonesia, SBY told Netherland first that their bilateral investment treaty will end in the middle of 2015, it was not mean that off investment but renew again together with China, France, Singapore and UK. In same occasion, SBY spoke out against UK owned Mining Company in Indonesia for 1 billion compensation cost. While SBY never raised the compensation payment over US$ 1 million for West Papuan from the LNG and Freeport Mc Moran in order to get more social security benefit. President Indonesia forgets what

West Papuan needs and aspiration for their social security benefit claim is symbol of marginalisation and discrimination.

Indonesia also never stops to influence Melanesian Countries in spite of those nations not being a signatory party for the 2504 resolution; some Melanesian nation defends Indonesian sovereignty but is normal in the international political interaction as state member. On the other hand, Melanesian countries have a moral obligation to help West Papuan independence. These four Melanesian nations have a strong reason if they want to bring to the ICJ to ask legal opinion on the political status on the West Papua territory because they were not state party to ratify this awful international resolution of the 2504.

1. Indonesia-Papua New Guinea. As the neighbouring partners always have higher degree in sustainable cooperation efforts on relation to focal point matter of West Papuan independence aspiration. Their bilateral agreement concentrates on territorial sovereignty, free zone trade, political asylum, border conflict, economic development and corporation in numerous occasions. They made border security and free trade zone agreement in 2002. It caused several realities, firstly a war between Indonesian army and pro-independence groups after which 10.000 Papuans fled to PNG, then found OPM/TPN central base in the border in 1960s and early 21 century many political activist escaped into border areas against back Indonesian border soldiers. In 2013 both the countries signed a Comprehensive Partnership with two indications that trade and investment interest in which defence free market system and defence territorial integrity on Western half of Papua New Guinea Island, West Papua not to support independence sovereignty.

   On 27 February 2015, new Indonesian foreign minister met Foreign Minister of Papua New Guinea. Their official bilateral meeting produced public statement on their bilateral cooperation agreement in the areas of territorial integrity, security and regional matter of MSG which was agreed by both foreign ministers. As an example of the result, the current shortage of two Indonesian by OPM/TPN in the border, Indonesia urged PNG to take responsibility to realise this two Indonesian from the hand of TPN then successfully realised when PNG troops deployed to the border. However, border conflict potentially increased many people's deaths and unnecessary murder and human rights violation will occur when three party agreements was not passed namely Indonesia, PNG and West Papua. Trilateral agreement is most essential to maintain peace and security in the border region because both the state cannot underestimate West Papua, in the practice West Papua is the one political actor since the mount of NLM.

2. Indonesia-Vanuatu bilateral agreement. They have reached joint communiqué on West Papua between Indonesian Foreign Minister and Vanuatu Foreign Minister, Moana Carcasses on 9 March 2004. They both have agreed about the importance of the comprehensive peaceful dialogue for settlement the conflict in West Papua, non-intervention and respects. Since Moana became Prime Minister, He has addressed peaceful political negotiation at UNGA in 2013 and Annual Meeting of Common Wealth Countries in the same year, how Indonesia reacted was no doubt, as no commitment was put into action according to the above bilateral treaty agreed. Indonesian has promised to provide $US20 million for Cyclone Pam victim reconstruction and rehabilitation projects while West Papuan fundraisers were killed by INP in Wamena District, but West Papuan never been stops to raise money to help their Melanesian brother and sisters in Vanuatu. Indonesia use this natural disaster moment for gaining Vanuatu government but it was difficult to convince because the Vanuatu government

was under John Natumen, who strongly backs independence movement.

3. Indonesia-Solomon Islands Relationship. Their bilateral agreement was signed after the 21 century since West Papuan independence became regional matters at MSG. On 28 February 2015, Indonesian foreign minister visited Honiara. In the bilateral meeting between Indonesia Foreign Minister H.E. Retno L.P. Marsudi and Solomon Island foreign Minister Hon. Milner Tozaka MP, their press statement highlighted some areas including stronger cooperation, relationship and people to people contact. They agreed to education, visa arrangement, exchange information, education and economic development and most importantly give a greater Indonesian's engagement at the regional affairs at the MSG. Three aspects in relation to West Papua affairs; *by people to people contacts* can involve money politics, pay off Solomon Islands leaders especially policy makers; Indonesia can take over economic activities in Solomon Island, Indonesia can lead to dictate their regional policy at the MSG in particular case.

Indonesia and Solomon Islands bilateral ties can be changed anytime. Current Prime Minister, Menaseh Sogavere, in his Chairmanship of MSG became strongly backed as ULMWP obtained an observer member at the MSG and endorsing forum observer for PIF in 2015. That not only stops at this stage but most vitally pushes West Papua back to decolonisation desk for independence according to his media statement during the PIF meeting in Port Moresby.

4. Indonesia-Fiji Arrangement. Their ties are deeper and closely measured to other Melanesian countries basically in some strategic areas, such as security, investment and development aspects based on mutual respect on territorial integrity. On 1 March 2015, Indonesia Foreign Minister Retno Marsudi and Fiji Foreign Minister Ratu Inoke made public statement that they agreed to stronger

cooperation for UN peace keeping that Indonesia provided peace keepers training course in Jakarta. Melanesian Country of Fiji dislikes seeing what's happing in their Melanesian fellows' murders under Indonesian military government. Rationally it does not make sense how Indonesia provides peace keepers training, while Indonesia itself has a very bad military record in the world. They were also applauded since their trade and investment agreement made in 2000s have reached up to US $ 26.2 million. It was widely criticised that both Fiji and Indonesia have experienced bad record in their military ruling government, which created a huge violence and conflict tension in last severe years in the Asia Pacific Region.

Their ties were also maintained by various opportunities regionally and internationally. When Fiji founded the PIDF, Indonesia became partner member in their young age almost two years old, even Indonesia is part member of the G77 nations which was led by Fiji. In the nature of the IGO, normally they agreed to series of good plan and program to deliver and tackle out their social and economic development challenges, political and environmental barriers bilaterally and multilaterally. This is the moment when Indonesian behaviour can show that sometimes it closes off when it comes to the case of West Papua. Whether in the PIDF and or G77, the state leader discusses on multiple problems, Indonesia sometime uses West Papua's social reality as an example to promote better development for all islands within Indonesia rule except the issue related to sovereignty and integrity.

Indonesia has plans to terminate more than 60 foreign investment treaties and has renewed it in the middle of 2015. Before SBY left from his position he pointed out that the investment and trade sector to be one of the prime agenda for next president of Indonesia. Current president, Jokowi background from entrepreneurship, in his political campaign promised to look more into internal affairs rather than outside but it was just a buzz word, Indonesia cannot grow their domestic economy without foreign investments. Even without foreign partners, the poverty burden of over 300 million Indonesian population will not get eradicated, private foreign investment is the alternative capital such compensation, dividend and tax revenue are potential resources to distribute low income family.

B. MULTILATERAL AGREEMENTS

Multilateral agreement was made between Indonesia and multilateral governmental organisation in relation with West Papua's resources in the early 21st century. Indonesia made cooperation with these multilateral governmental bodies such as UN, EU, APEC, PIF, G20 and OPEC. West Papuan nationalist confronts them as their multilateral cooperation goals are not always positive development and sometimes very higher negative risks to threat native Papuan society in the reality; exploitation of the rich resources without benefit for native Papuan; creating potential conflict region due to the greedy rich region; gaining their common benefit for money and power, nothing in their arrangement provides a golden opportunity for West Papuan except political development initiatives. The multilateral agreement contains non-intervention in the domestic political affairs; it is desperately looking after the illegal resolution of the 2405. It's very critical though that the multilateral government and Indonesia have wrongly introduced non-intervention policy to undermine international treaties and covenant on the treatment of West Papua in the name of a new world order and entire global plans, they lack credibility to the West Papuan.

1. Indonesia-EU Relationship multilaterally has more significance in the 21st century. On the same day of Indonesia's illegal integration of West Papua territory, the 1st May of 2014 signed their first Partnership and Corporation Agreement (PCA) between

Indonesia and European Union on trades and human rights after the 16 EU parliament members passed recommendation in two significant point that ban arm trades and human rights protection on 26 March 2014 in Brussels. In the same year on 8 December the extra judicial killing happened again in Paniai, EU showed no sign of action. It couldn't find positive effect of EU engagement to Indonesia on human rights, human security and democracy. That is the real reality how their agreement was made in the name of human rights. Using the name of human rights, peace and justice on their multilateral arrangement created huge human rights abuses again and again in opposition.

2. Indonesia -PIF Relationship. Indonesia became PIF in 2002; it is one of Indonesia's victorious moments as it knocked off regional attention. Regional wisdom and recognition on the West Papuan defeated by Indonesian membership status on behalf of Native People. PIF had offered a regional dialogue in peace settlement for this slow armed conflict pacific territory in 2004, however, Indonesia constantly rejected it. According to PIF and Indonesian cooperation was formed in 2000, since then it was formally accepted as dialogue partner member, fully backing Indonesian colonial policy of special autonomy not support to separatist movement. In their agreement West Papuan was not allowed to participate except Indonesian officials, although MRP had recognised West Papuan representative body under PIF administration.

In connection to West Papua's current affairs for PIF, several PIF leaders expressed their strong voice to human rights improvement, from their 2006 communiqué agreed to uphold human rights for all residents in Papua and unsettle root cases need to be ended in peaceful way. After 9 years of being voiceless on that matter, their special regional committee brought up to leaders table as one of five priority agenda in the leaders' summit 2015. As Indonesian reaction warned PIF leaders not to mention and support West Papuan independence struggle, the leaders were reinstated to respect Indonesian sovereignty, but for human rights they cannot leave it because West Papua is pacific regional community as they were obligate to look after. Then PIF new Chair, PNG Prime Minister, Piter was asked to have a consultation with Indonesia before pacific regional fact finding mission was sent.

3. Indonesia-APEC Multilateral Relation. This Rich Natural Resource Melanesian Territory of West Papua (RNRMTWP) is located at the central regional economic business area between Pacific and Asian country's border line, that's why Indonesian role in the APEC is very influential. In 2010, all the heads of states signed a multilateral agreement on APEC Multi Year Plan on Infrastructure Development and Investment; they have agreed to establish a Public-Private Partnership Centre in Indonesia with implementation term 2013-2016. Indonesia became APEC investment central city; Indonesia will search private finance in this project as recommended by APEC leaders in accordance to their multilateral agreement. What will happen, Indonesia could be seeking the financial aid from more than 100 MNCs who operates legally and illegally in West Papua territory to boost their future investment benefit. Logically, Indonesian government can do bargain by granting extra hectares for concession areas as one warranty if those MNCs financing the establishments of PPPC.

In the foreign investment forum, president Jokowi attended the APEC meeting in China 2014. CEO leaders applauded his first time speech about New Indonesia President without text. He spoke short and simple words but meaningful one and was stimulating for their multilateral agenda. This multilateral governmental organisation had not shown any reaction on the root problems which is social security and human rights impact of their economic activities in the past years. President Joko was open heart about allowing foreign investments into his country. He never missed to address those social security barriers which were faced by his nation, and also about real outcome of the higher foreign investment present in these rich islands of nation.

4. Indonesia and G20 Multilateral Ties. Indonesia signed multilateral agreement with G20 in 1999. Why Indonesia is a G20 member in relation to West Papua? Read the answers: West Papua claimed to contribute 70% of rich natural resources (Gold, Natural Gas, Copper, Timber etc.) while 30% from other region in Indonesia; over 100 MNCs in operating, Indonesia wanted to share these rich resources in order to block off the G20 members' support for the West Papua's independence plea. The establishment of this multilateral organisation was primarily effected by the East Asian financial crisis in 1998. From Indonesian perspective it was tremendous misallocation of foreign financial aid, which was spent for military operation into East Timor, West Papua, Maluku and Aceh. The main goal of G20 Summit 2014 platform is *investment and infrastructure by increased private sector participation*, this strategy is not new in IPE practices it likely will not ensure global economic justice, wants more capitalist profit. MNCs desperately were intervened in domestic politics within Indonesia and how West Papuan gets benefit from it, indeed unfortunate.

The G20 meeting in Australia after a month of new Indonesian president took place at office. Some capitalist nation leaders were influenced with the president Widodo, as he had his personal profession from the middle class entrepreneurship or middle business owner in Jakarta. His speech similar to APEC, invites capitalist nations to make investments in his country, one of them include Indonesia navy transportation and mega railway projects that can cost million to billion dollars. The leaders agreed to infrastructure the project privately involving their final communiqué especially to third world member countries of G20 like Indonesia. From the year of G20 in 1999, many private companies are willing to invest their capital in RNRTWP.

5. Indonesia and OPEC. Indonesia is one of the biggest gas and oil export country because of RNRTWP. Indonesian national rate for Oil is assumed to be 50% who contributed by two provinces in West Papua that is why Indonesia became members of OPEC. Despite withdrawing in 2008, until now Indonesia remains to be the fourth world's largest LNG exporter in global market in 2013. On March 2014 U.S. Energy Information Administration reported that potential LNG's revenue comes from West Papua by BP LNG Tangguh Project. Indonesia will increase LNG export rate in order validate again its membership at the OPEC in coming years.

6. Indonesia-UN Agencies Cooperation. The Government of Indonesia and United Nations Development Programme signed mutual agreement cooperation in the realisation of MDGs. First agreement was made in 2001, first phase from 2001-2005, second phase 2006-2010, third phase 2011-2015.They also made agreement in term of UNDP assistance for Indonesian Government's medium term development 2004-2009 and continued next term between 2010-2014. UNDP has entered into an agreement with Indonesia for basic agreement of technical assistance signed in 29 October 1954, agreement on special fund signed in 17 October 1960 and operational assistance agreement signed in 12 June in 1969. Long term UNDP operation in Indonesia and UNDP office did not establish in two provinces in West Papua Territory.

II. FOREIGN AID PRACTICES

The FA is an important component of development discourse under new world system in the post-second world war (Underhill 2007). Philosophically, FA was derived from humanitarian bound wherein the colonialist states must pay back moral obligation to their ex-colony countries or territories by funding post-colonial development plan for the better development. FA theories in the contemporary world was discussed, many theorists classified six common aspects as humanitarian, subsistence, military, bribery, prestige, and economic development. The common requirements faced by countries and territories of potential matters include *human rights abuses, guerrilla war, humanitarian crisis, marginalisation, cultural and ethnical genocide and multiple development problems.* Then West Papua is unquestionably is eligible territory for these FA operations.

Indonesia is biggest MBFA recipient country assumed over hundreds billion US dollars in history. MBFA granted to Indonesia consists of three reasons such as big population with higher poverty standards, global security and political economic benefit. The economy growth, agricultural, education, health, social, transport, energy, urban development and infrastructure were disadvantages even the global era today. The reason why this condition is the dilemma in development practices. One of barriers is huge corruption in the government officials (Cookson 2008) despite UN and National Corruption Office working on to combat corruption; it had not met the good outcome due to its bureaucracy complication. One good suggestion, it would be more effective if the Acronyms of KKN (Collusion, Corruption, Nepotism) attitudes are eradicated it. Indonesian official within two provinces found corruptors, Papuan official learned and experienced by Indonesian KKN tradition, law enforcement weakened, and central government authority to control corruptor in West Papua was impracticable and Jakarta funded opportunity cost far higher to encounter the separatism matter.

Restriction for foreign NGOs operates in the conflict territory, this must be caused by several factors; firstly avoiding their contribution and interference for separatist movement like experience other conflict countries around the world; secondly it can impact for their domestic NGOs growth in taking responsibility in the foreign project; the local and national NGOs mostly support national interest; foreign NGOs can have the capacity to direct engagement with affected people; foreign NGOs will sometimes take over all the projects both funded by foreign aid and domestics with professional report. Some foreign NGOs are still operating but they are not significantly helping Papuan community, reporting and collecting factual data is also very difficult to found out. Despite several UN status NGOs; New Zealand Oxfam in Nabire region, International Red Cross and WWF in Jayapura being long time operation, they have poor report, even so these only concern the social and economic development not social and political violence. It absolutely has not matched their report about the effect of slow armed conflict in their deployment unlike in Congo, Burma and Afghanistan.

UN Coordinating Body is based in Jakarta not in West Papua. These UN office dysfunctions in terms of dissemination of the factual information on the foreign aid projects failures and challenges in its implementation. How many foreign aid partner organisations are based in West Papua and what difficulty they are facing? There are severe international development agencies such as UNDP and World Bank, UNICEF, WHO. No one is interested in doing research or writing books about the FA in West Papua, only reports or articles comments on the media or internet. There is a need to have deeper analysis on the FA implementation on whether there are any advantages or disadvantages; from the academic work will it be able to help in making recommendation and suggestion in terms of seeking solution.

In fact, three major types of FA are found to be delivering in the region. They are multilateral, official bilateral and unofficial aid.

II.1. MULTILATERAL AID

Multilateral aid donors was started in Papua since 1960-an. Fund for the Development of West Irian was funded to *Free Act of Choice* in 1969 under United Nations Executive Administration but since 1970s it was replaced into Indonesian rule. After 21st century Indonesian government via his open door foreign policy agreed that only world development agencies can strictly enter into this conflict territory for FA projects, those are UNESCO, UNICEF, World Bank, IMF, ADB, WHO and UNDP. They are also part of stakeholder for MDGs projects, Jakarta Central government's rule that required not dealing with war affected West Papuan civilians. In 2006, The World Bank reported that 73 per cent of its 2.6 million inhabitants live below the poverty line, social and human indicators remain far behind other provinces, with poor health care, high rates of infant, maternal mortality and prevalent levels of HIV/AIDS, and low literacy and numeracy rate. In 2015, Australian Council for Education Research (ACER) had undertaken research for two years and found that lack of ADB aid implementation, then positively ACER promised to recommend ABD for IT development assistance in West Papua for secondary school level, however it will not guarantee upon its propose.

World Bank and IMF, these two international financial institutions structurally and systematically intervene foreign financial aid operation in the country, provides soft loan credit but it is limited to West Papuan access to get social economy benefit from it. For the sake of local people, World Bank and IMF bring financial aid for their social economic development, humanitarian aid by providing money for household because of financial crisis. Because of many multilateral development agencies present in the conflict region, many West Papuan people have misconception on it; but in reality their disadvantage will be advantage, their aspiration and desires will be heard, their needs will be satisfied, their political independence demand will go away from them, their suffering, victims, violence, war and conflict will come to an end because of them. Furthermore, they still have issues that their original West Papuan currency possibly has to be validated again through IMF and World Bank because special autonomy law allows them to maintain their West Papuan national identity such as morning star flag, currency gulden and national anthem. All of the above concepts became unpromising for their national identity building like the currency because in the special autonomy law, the financial and monetary system is under central government of Jakarta controls unlike Aceh, where they have their own currency or not. If in the special autonomy law has content financial and monetary affairs which are fully responsible by West Papuan, there is any possibility to reactivate the old currency or create new currency through World Bank and IMF authority why not. IMF granted loan US$5 billion to the government of Indonesia in 2001. This money was misused by Indonesia for their military occupation sending 30.000 Special Forces (Kopasus) in Aceh and West Papua resulting in Chief Theys Eluay, the PPC leader being found in dead 2002. Multilateral financial aid unquestionably allocates into encountering and chasing West Papuan independence leaders.

What is the UN agencies role in dealing with multilateral aid in West Papua? Financial aid is totally not involved and technical aid is always involved, UN agencies are not multilateral financial aid donor but their core role as development consultant. How much money from provincial budget is going to their account for consideration to the budget allocating into foreign NGOs, local migrant owned NGOs and Native owned NGOs? Lack of partnership with local community groups the aid ineffectively delivered and misrepresentation by

Indonesian owned NGOs. The real consequences has to take place where marginalisation, hunger and poverty, violence and illiteracy standard still remains higher. According to HDI report that in many aspects very low standards while foreign aid index are higher. Thousand local community groups have been discriminated by the Indonesian foreign aid delivery system, empowerment of local community groups was done only in their policy paper but not in practise, West Papuan people distrusts new Indonesian national program " *by people to people contacts* " development model under new government today.

Pacific regional governmental organisation of PIF granted a foreign aid packet for regional stability and integrity by funding million dollars, initiated to provide a better security for their native pacific community in West Papua from the war and violence. It looks like a good plan for human security in spite of the realisation desperately is unusable. Individual country's aid like second powerful nation of PIF, New Zealand has second biggest security aid to Indonesia after Australia, the military and police equipment's and training funding billion dollars. New Zealand's aid to Indonesia critically rose when some parliament members and NGOs called to end military ties with Indonesia after mass killing took place in Paniai on 8 December 2014. Foreign aid on conflict resolution remains strong by pacific civil society groups; they request New Zealand government to find political ways to resolve the case rather than social and economic development. The security or military aid is more helpful if it proposes to establish a real peace and real stability in the region, West Papuan beacon hope that how New Zealand uses its non-permanent security seat at UN 2015-2016 is to promote real freedom from Indonesian security force operation.

European Union is biggest multilateral donator for West Papuan project in Indonesia but APEC is only economy forum not concerned with the humanitarian projects. Multi billion dollars from EU going to Indonesian pocket on behalf of West Papuan humanitarian crisis. APEC's weakness never empowers local business and social security protection in local and national level. Looking at their investment for growth, their social responsibility as multilateral agency dislikes maintaining the economic and social rights for citizen. Local business empowerment plan does not enhance West Papuan local business needs, migrant business and global business owner growing vastly. Dr Benny Giay, a well-known West Papuan religious leader said that all business sectors even the Churches are biased by migrants everywhere in our rich land, we have no hope, place to survive our business for lifetime. Whether God is injustice to see people tears or foreigners created this rich land to take over by them to harvest entire rich resources.

APEC, EU and Indonesia were never interested to empower local business owners to take over in business sector at all level; small, medium, and large in West Papua. Take an example; West Papuan Arabica Coffee from Moanemani village went to European Market before the 21st century, this local production coffee was the luckiest local product in the international global market as it became lucrative business. 35 years director experience; Ir Didimus Tebay, a first West Papuan degree in Agriculture, Agronomy from the social economy agriculture program said "I became very stupid educated man in Satan cycle situation from the first president until current president of Indonesia, multilateral foreign aid and multilateral economic business institution must to stimulate our local economic business to growth, provide some government aid for running to expand our business in local and national and international market."

II.2. OFFICIAL BILATERAL AID

An official bilateral aid donor from the first world countries is high in relation to West Papua. FA is the promoter of international peace and prosperity through developing cordial relations between donor and recipient countries but also foreign aid policy as tool to promote national interest of donor countries (Morgan et al 2006). Many donor countries expected their funding to be used for good development in some crucial program of good government, better democracy and conflict prevention, the situations has not yet improved the corruption, killings, abuses with slow armed conflict is still invisibly enduring taking years and years unless resolve. If donor countries more defend their own political economic interest it will weaken the control of the aid effectiveness and implementation. Discrimination policy in foreign education scholarship appeared when the eligibility criteria is to study abroad directed to donor countries, to make investment to givers country, secondly most seriously given a priority for Indonesian student in the name of West Papuan.

University education project for West Papuan was funded by overseas donors; they are now developing in very low number of Papuan students. It is found that some core barriers are Indonesian student take on behalf of West Papuan, national procedure limitation and donor's countries weakness for their effective and control by this circumstance unworkable to enhance human resources development to marginalised West Papuan people. Writer met some Indonesian student in Australia during his study period 2009-2011 at Victoria University Melbourne; Writer asked them how did you get study here? They said we are on behalf of the Papuan student under Australian Scholarship Program AusAid because Papuan student failed to meet English test and general knowledge test. Writer actively contacted Papuan students who wanted to study abroad, their English very fluent considered to Indonesian student who met them at university. According to research shown 15,000 Indonesian students studying in Australia 2011 were only less than 5 students from West Papuan equal cases in USA, European countries, Japan and China.

Mostly official foreign military aid always had been misapplying. Scholars and activists assumed that by empowering these foreign military aid Indonesian forces attacking the native Papuan independence activist, protect their multinational gas and gold company concession areas, and sometimes they deny landowner compensation payment (Maire, 2010). Foreign financial aid heavily funded from US, Australia, British, Russia and EU nations while political instability and injustice is more solid case, thus West Papuan critical suggests that the aid must stop it and seek political solution. Many peace beloved people demand the foreign peace keeping force to control security tension, which is crucially significant for stabilisation and normalisation in order to foreign aid operation effectives like many conflict regions experience. On February 2015, Indonesian National Army, General Commander XVII Cendrawasih, Grasen G Siahaan confirmed that a new Indonesian Military Command will establish in Arfai about 40 hectares before 2016 and provincial budget will allocate it. Two critical points that firstly placed is historical place where TPN/OPM is first based location, secondly escalation military personnel who will make the war against TPN. The construction cost expenses is estimated to be very high, then it indicates that the foreign aid money will be spent through local government authority. The foreign financial aid for poverty and hungry reduction automatically will deficit because of the provincial fund allocating for this massive military project, the above is one example.

Foreign Aid aimed to tackle the world's most vulnerable society groups is virtual path to eradicate the worst situation whether of the independent states or not independent territories does not matter. Smith 2011 argued that the war and political unrest made very worst condition of mostly fragile states especially badly affected to the people under foreign rule. Commontly stated that foreign donors bilaterally has been growing to improve state nation building needs in particular potential donors like USAID, AusAID, Canadian Government, Norway and New Zealand. Indonesia is the biggest donor recipient country has seen helped in their national building since independence. It was a great opportunity and contributes a positive direct impact from the foreign aid except disadvantage groups from NSGT within Indonesia challenging by procedure limitation and discrimination. If Foreign Aid goes through West Papua, politically and economically higher risk for Indonesian integrity; many West Papuan study abroad gain good momentum for promoting independence aspiration and get more education. It can improve social and economic development and more encouraged thinking about real independence to become their self-government not special autonomy model and also against all MNCs like Freeport McMoran.

II.3. UNOFFICIAL BILATERAL AID

Unofficial bilateral aid is directed to government and NGOs in the recipient country of Indonesia. These foreign aid projects is channelled through NGO groups, often in the form of block grants for Papua funded by Oxfam groups joined with Dutch Protestant Church development organisation and Bread for the World. A number of other block funding agencies operated around the Indonesia on behalf of West Papua project, the local community groups became powerless to control, all of them centralised in Jakarta, the problem was that a native owned NGOs/CSOs lost opportunity to delivery foreign aid project for provide better service their people in the remote areas around the region.

There are groups of local NGOs emerging in all sectors from human security, environmental, health to human rights. Provincial government and Central government distrust the local NGOs; Indonesian government bureaucracy is dirty and unwise, prejudice in wrong way for their citizen participation in the national building and regional building like separatism, terrorism and criminalist. For West Papua such discrimination, marginalisation, stereotype are like stupid or Stone Age, state enemy are part of their daily life, the Indonesian government and migrant community have been doing it continuingly. The world is watching what the local people and NGOs have disadvantaged and disempowered by the government of Indonesia. Unofficial bilateral aid is channelled directly through local government or regency government in several places. Civil society groups also distrust central government and provincial government on unofficial bilateral aid from outside. Bureaucracy limitation and corruption is the two main factors, ordinary people distrust governmental official, and the old style of up down policy for developments is still being used. Jokowi President of Indonesia currently mentioned that people in West Papua have distrust towards their leaders in the bureaucracy level. Trust building is key dilemma, people of West Papua have experienced and threatened badly in the name of foreign aid, therefore they want that foreign aid to come through after regaining independence of West Papua, ordinary people and some migrant together with freedom fighters demand their independence sovereignty plea.

II.4. WHY FA NOT DELIVERED NATIONAL LIBERATION MOVEMENT

Growing number of the NLM around the globe were traced various critical notion with regards to the delivery system of the foreign aid. Normally those NLM's principle ideology is generated to sustain the international law of external rights to self- determination and UNGA resolution of 1514. Then NLM in West Papua has committed by a non-violent struggle approach to fight their political sovereign rights. The foreign government aid system critically remarked everywhere so that it is vitally re-considered in the global government order. Structurally, multilateral government is made and maintains international system including the freedom of movement and freedom of association while the NLM respects international values for Charter, Covenant and Resolution. The core point they argued is that whether any proper system or rule should be created to ensure foreign financial aid work is touchable with respect to legitimate NLM groups in each corner of the planet. Theoretical persuasion of the NLM groups are part of international political community groups, if their fundamental principles are to support global goal of justice, peace and freedom, by all political entities involvement to be driving force and is workable of world provision to enhance stronger partnership for good mutual interest toward world peace and justice agenda itself.

Without offering humanitarian aid to the people at the NLM groups the common principle of human rights and humanitarian values is unworkable. To create a tolerable policy for humanitarian bound would be better in sense of how international government sets up a new paradigm in terms of humanitarian work system for the stabilisation and normalisation of the world conflict on the ground. Administering power or state members must endorse security and peace ethics and norms rather than national sovereignty interests and militaristic loom; hence, a critical suggestion is the UNSC potentially must play a monitoring role on ensuring the global rule. The war is unfinishable business in our global world today, if UNSC or international security resolution is more defensive it will be more difficult and in the final outcome the conflict will never end. Learn case studies from Afghanistan, Congo and others, UNSC defensive resolution truly denied international principle of human rights law where International Joint Force or Peace Keeping Force involved in murdering many civilian and NLM fighter in the fact.

Writer argued about what is important, the FA must deliver to this group of people; critically provide some rational ideas with respects to all the governmental bureaucratic stage:

a. The groups of NLM are not terrorist group or international public enemy.

b. This group respects and maintains the world obligation on peace and justice.

c. This group of people are human being; humanitarian aid must deserve them.

d. NLM principally fight for their minority rights and political sovereignty rights.

e. NLM sustain support the realization of international program and UN charter, covenant and treaties.

f. NLM are not public enemy or not enemy for civilian, only enemy for colonialist government and its military for better change.

The UNSC always is very weaker to classify these insurgencies characters to correctly judge them according to constructive procedural manners. There is fundamental explanation of the international relation theory to classify international political actor particularly non-state actor who gives positive effect and contribution on its international peace and security. NLM is one of them, it is definitely wrong if OPM/TPN are categorised into terrorism and criminal groups. UNSC and UNGA must do more closer approach with them, what the NLM has been doing for West Papua is absolutely maintained in international obligation and norms in advocating their independence sovereignty rights, they are asking for the UNTEA and UNSF reactivate again in the territory. Secretary General can look back at the past of UN failure, it should not ask state members mandate, Secretary General can use his good office the UN authority to establish again two UN main bodies in the Melanesian territory of West Papua.

The global system of the humanitarian aid must equally get good human security services such as all the society in our planet is part of world community groups. In 2000 former UN Secretary General, Kofi Anan, declared human security principle the endorsement for fulfilling human needs of development. Foreign government action is obviously inconsistent, the global justice values dead, distrust the factual situation that are reported by civil society and NGOs and Faith groups. The critical condition was natural disaster relief funding from foreign donators did not meet OPM/TPN members and civilian around the areas because they are sufferers and true victims of this bloody disaster. Losing their lifetime and wishes: soul and assets. More than 100.000 civilian and guerrilla fighters are in the jungle, who has never been threatened via foreign humanitarian aid. The character of insurgencies groups of the OPM/TPN is unlike Congo, Afghanistan, Burma or other conflict regions around the globe. International human security resolution needs to be taken place in terms of settling a long silent armed war between Pro-Indonesian Armed Groups versus Pro-West Papuan Independence Armed Groups.

III. WORLD GLOBAL AGENDA

World Global development programs have common responsibility to serve all nations, people and territories on the earth planet not only one particular groups of country. No one is perfect nation, people and territory in our bloody world, and then global plan must render equitable manners. Writer strongly differs in the conceptual and practical understanding of the definition of Global South vs. Global North, Western versus Eastern nations because it has defined them into systematic structural discrimination in our one world, if we all wander to create our better world itself. With respect to state nations building, writer strongly agrees with state nation's classification such as developed nations, developing nations, underdeveloping nations, poor nations and disadvantage nations. Now West Papua is being colonised by underdeveloped nation of Indonesia, according to human development index by World Bank in 2010. Indonesia is still in underdeveloped nations category, from this worst condition we can take a rational argumentation that

Indonesia will never develop West Papuan lifestyle, in the reality found marginalisation and systematic genocide happening in the 21st century, whatever the 21st century of global plan application for West Papua will not meet in improving social economy and other development program barriers according to native West Papuan expectation.

Definition of the first world, second world, third world and fourth world nations is also considered to lead discriminating each other in the name of competition and power interest. Some Western writer stated that fourth world nations are indigenous nation groups, however fourth world definition strongly disagree, therefore, writer introduces a new definition of Lost World Nations (LWN). It will shape to provide a critical argumentation about why it is called as the lost world nations. LWN is derived from current social realities of systematic and structural genocide in many life sectors across the religion, racial, cultural and tradition, and facing human made disaster region like impact of the climate change; increasing sea level. The sustainable colonialism from the first, second and third world nations is undeniably seems to be a massive hell weapon for genocide people of the LWN. Systematic killings of the LWN people and expanding systematic global hegemony are another form of colonisation itself in the 21st century. All the circumstances clearly refers to disappearance in certain time and year. LWN groups already missing in their some aspect such as their motherland, mother tongue, tribes, clan and population, believe system, lost freedom and independence, everlasting peace, harmony and justice. Today global mechanism in relation to re-creation of all those who has lost human life aspects absolutely will not help out, there is zero rule of law and less legal authority to reinforce international law on indigenous rights. Discovery rule in the international system is totally against native or indigenous rights in conceptual and practical realities, it already became debatable matter at the World Indigenous Forum.

III.1. DEMOCRACY AND GOOD GOVERNMENT DEVELOPMENT

Global democracy and political development provision became urgent demand in relation to potential ongoing matters in the troubled regions of the planet. Importance of democracy improvement was overwhelmingly asked for Indonesia, since freedom of expression and freedom of movement was banned by the state authority. Domestic political instability and military operation endured less intention from the global multilateral governmental institutions for monitoring. UN agencies help to maintain world obligation of democracy and good government projects, UNDP takes over by providing financial and technical assistance. The 15 years operation has not improved; it has seen failure of these global agencies in their endorsement and effectiveness in investigation. What can UNDP do if the freedom of expression for political opinion is unprotected? The Jakarta's worrying provides an open democracy due to political sentiments of the independence movement of West Papua. As a result the outcome is the murder of activists has been on the rise, however, the global government agencies never reports this as a proof of no democracy crisis.

UN agencies and FA agencies failures are commonly criticised upon their role for democracy work. The impediments; firstly has no strong commitment, no engagement into core conflict parties, lack of network, education and investigation, national authority bans foreign investigation on political unrest. Democracy development is not enough for bureaucracy level; underground society must be given opportunity to meet this common goal as pluralist society in Indonesia. Non-state actor proactively working into support global democracy plan, West Papuan is rejecting the Indonesia special autonomy and a new policy of UP4B became target for murdering because of prejudice of separatism sentiment such as extrajudicial killings for independence leader of Mako Tabuni and several activist, same experience to pro-independence leader, Theodorus Eluway. There was kidnapping by special force in 2001 when he rejects the special autonomy in the meantime. The lack of global government endorsement and monitoring of the democracy development and even reporting became key turmoil; West Papuan gave distrust to the UN development agencies in operating into trouble Melanesian region. Those West Papuan leaders were killed by Indonesian force became a true global democracy fighter in the 21st century as they were involved in maintaining an open democracy in Indonesia.

Indonesian constitution chapter 28 ensures that there is freedom of movement or gathering and freedom of speech to freely express political opinion publicly and the international community appreciated out went present of Indonesia, SBY has successfully maintained global provision on the pure democracy principles. His promise on the improvement of better or open democracy into two Indonesian conflict provinces in West Papua territory through open dialogue or whatever approaches was only undermined by the international public tension. Greater global community criticism that special autonomy policy has failed to make a positive advantage specifically to ensure civil society participation rights in public policy making. Obviously, new unit of acceleration of development for Papua and Papua Barat Province was made without any West Papuan people's involvement. Same things were made to the special autonomy rule formulation previously even no public consultation to relevancy global institution of UNDP in the formulation and production stages.

International policy on indigenous rights is not applicable law. Indonesian government has adopted the law of political protection for Indigenous minority rights. Whatever the colonialist government law and policies are never content with freedom expression on a right to self–determination for native people and in their law application. In 2008, Tepius Tabuni was shot dead by police in Wamena during a peaceful protest on the celebration of world indigenous days on 9 of September. The raising flag of UNs and Indonesian alongside with West Papua morning star flag in the meantime as form of inauguration for the 100.000 native population deaths during 32 military dictatorship president of Indonesia. Without feeling fear freely, over thousand Papuan have a moment for declaration of political rights by using world commemoration time to convey their voice of grief and future destiny did not meet what their desired since there was massive attack by Indonesian coalition troops; mobile police and special force. Multilateral government of United Nations indigenous committee was unable to investigate the incident, even national and international government have no action on that despite local NGOs or CSOs and political-social groups hugely demanding an international investigation team to advocacy this emergency of crime against humanity and brutality.

The global policy of good democracy development unlikely has seen a better improvement under SBY regime despite severe international government were given a big applauding for this little achievement. Evidently, some conflict provinces challenged to struggle poor democracy system since the new era of democracy transformation especially politically disadvantage region can be good evidence to know what Indonesian democracy looks like. Two potential conflict provinces in West Papua, Maluku, Aceh and others have faced worst experience during a new order regime definitely very strictly control military rule on people's political expression and good will towards political stabilisation and development always been denied, at least zero scale for foreign government attention. A good international reputation on the growing better democracy condition with today's Indonesian democratic government does not mean that this pure democracy was already accomplished to pay back of global demand.

The world democracy forums were several times held in Bali indirectly reminds Indonesia for greater democracy. Multilateral statement of the fourth Bali Democracy Forum in Nusa Dua, Bali 8-9 December 2011 has shown only theoretical rhetoric. President SBY stressed by his words that *"democracy must include efforts to systematically provide built-in protection of human rights must be coupled with tolerance and rule of law. Furthermore, he said, as people rights declaimed more political space and greater participation in the determination of their future, effective governance needs the support of civil society"*. Australian representative also strongly encouraged civil society participation on democracy. Nevertheless, three West Papuan protesters were detained when they jump inside the Australia consulate during BDF held in 2012. Australia broke the international obligation to protect them from Indonesia brutality; Indonesia broke the promise of the importance of civil society contribution on democracy itself.

Now coming to the new president of Jokowi, He has promised at the public eyes for open talk or dialogue, it seemly difficult to articulate from his language whether it is part of his agenda for real democracy development in Indonesia or not. New Indonesian president is likely to beacon hope for West Papuan demands who assumed by many people. Most people who trust him in democracy development will guarantee freedom of expression and movement. During his first Christmas visit to capital city of Papua province said *if feeling of trust between people and leaders built then communication easily to conduct, the communication can be one direction but also two direction dialogues. All problems can solve in conjunction with dialogue, dialogue can be short and long. Open dialogue. All must want dialogue, talking people. Because of talk it is we can know what its root case is. I do not want arguing matter, I want solve mater. But I am sure with a dialogue praise can short; the case can solve said President.* Some critics say that Jokowi plans for open dialogue for economic social development and environmental not for political status of the West Papua territory and will not be fair if it fails to meet what West Papuan wants. The dialogue mechanism must be clear before it will hold; for West Papuan prospective simply offering for internationally mediated dialogue or third party mediated dialogue is the final option.

III.2. HUMAN RIGHTS AND HUMANITARIAN DEVELOPMENT

Human rights development agenda is a suitable method to maintain the HRL in accordance to UN Charter and principle, every people and nations around the world in particular colonized or marginalized minority people does not matter whether they are under the other colonial power. All the state members uphold world obligation in realization the HRL provision such after several years Indonesian signed the International declaration of universal HRL in 1948; this great program completely did not work to protect and respect the fundamental HRL for West Papuan. Because the second president of Indonesia announced a priority program of military operation based around the villages in West Papua after Dutch left from the country 1960s, and 1966 Indonesia removed from state members at the UN since cold war with its hidden political initiative just took over West Papua. As a result of that massive human rights violation, more than 200.000 innocent native Papuan populations were hunted down under the big dictatorship of the Suharto regime. This bloody war was unknown to the outside world for almost half a century without foreign investigation and advocacy missions because foreign activists and journalists were banned access into regions under Indonesian national authority.

The huge escalation of ongoing human rights violation attracted an international alarm more than a decade after the 21st

century. In a small scale attention was developed to monitor the circumstances under UN auspice the trouble territory in 2012. The chief of Human Rights High Commission of the United Nations had strongly pushed Indonesia to maintain 180 point of Universal Periodic Review especially freedom of expression and freedom of movement on her visit in 12-13 November, in its recommendation and assessment she advised Indonesia needs to adopt these UPR point and do better treatment for all population in the West Papuan territory.

Under the new president Jokowi regime, a massive human rights violation has been occurring badly, therefore, the violence never stopped until the end of Indonesian colonialism. There are over hundreds human rights abuse cases after the Jokowi regime. From the new order regime to Jokowi regime today there is lack of UN Human Rights body entry to the region despite Jokowi promised for UN expert, foreign journalists for free advocacy to entry into this respective region. In the 2014-2015 found many cases it begun from a bloody murder for several students on 8th December in Paniai 2014, Killing of humanitarian fund raisers on April, Dead of a West Papuan and some heavily wounded in Puncak Jaya including killing of two students in Timika, Murdering of two people in Serui plus over 300 students in Java were arrested on the first December in 2015 on West Papuan independence celebration day. Which one the West Papuan will be killed in the future because of the independence aspiration is never and will ever stopped by this brutal action, the independence aspiration is the principle of human rights values to never give up for West Papuan and the independence aspiration already became a regional agenda of MSG. West Papuan diplomats will never stop to advocate every corner of the world for attracting more global society and international organisations reaction.

III.3. GLOBAL SECURITY

Traditionally a global security plan is derived from world mandate in maintaining international security and it has emerged again since criminalist and terrorist movement expanded worldwide. The key goal of the global security agenda is to counter world terrorism and to protect trouble nations from the war and violation by every nation state in the 21st century. Indonesia is one of targeted country of it when look at the application field it really complicated matter in conjunction with security tension in West Papua. Most of local respected churches, NGOs, social and political groups believed to this terrorist group have been working collaboratively with Indonesian military win to counter Papuan independence movement activity and human rights defenders. From many credible resources indicated 30% of foreign financial aid misallocation in funding sustainable military operation in West Papua. Despite Indonesia is a signatory nation for anti-global terrorism plan and proud of a top leader of Bin Laden killed by President Obama in 2012 but also Indonesia itself expand his terrorist networks everywhere as Islamic State.

This global security plan was solemnly delivered by regional government and powerful states via funding multi million dollars, the regional political groups of Pacific Island Forum was evolved in shifting financial aid including triple powerful leader of UNSC which are three veto rights states of USA, UK and China plus a non-permanent members of Australia 2013-2014 period heavily funded to support it. Each financial year reported out a funding of multiple million dollars for the pacific regional security instability. Current US navy based in Darwin protects the international and regional crime and terrorism but why Indonesia, China and Russia with their counterpart anti-capitalist countries responded hesitantly. Indonesian foreign policy experts argued that it's a sign of US and Australia's indirect intervention on the independence aspiration of West Papua. Many writers believe that, West Papuan people happy to see more AUS and

US based navy to come into West Papuan border on the sea. If US want to do direct intervention on the slow armed conflict, it is more helpful because terrorist movement already rooted into migrant community in the region, people of West Papua should be want to provide navy base land whether North or South Islands for global security purpose.

Border security and human security is two embedded factors whether it is part of plan into global security system or not, essentially it takes account into consideration. Internationalisation of the border conflict is a regional duty it not only is a bilateral concern between PNG and Indonesia, the nature of conflict always is a special feature in the global scheme. Due to political sentiment amongst the interested groups; native minority population and victims' community expressed a multilateral government intervention inquiry when the human security project was not implemented even with the UNCHR helping such many country, only a single UN agency is unable to tackle out the worst circumstances. A specialisation institution should be established and given more UN authority for accessibility.

Global political communities groups have been facing difficulty to identify slow armed war as non-international armed conflict. The new armed conflict is slowly increasing, internationalize and regionalize this armed conflict for wider attention will always be core barriers. Shootings in the border areas still continue and they are silently enduring in an uncertain time. A shooting incident between OPM led by General Matias Wenda evolved to Indonesian police chief in Papua shot and his body guarded in 2014. The president of Indonesia, Jokowi's priority plan is maritime state that returns their past policy in their old order regime or so called the Soekarno's era. Widodo's fundamental reasons behind are protecting their maritime sovereignty after crack down with Australia, protect illegal arm supply and protect foreign intervention on West Papua. This maritime policy was backed by former President Megawati's Party because of their internal political party interest to control power and the natural resources.

III.3.1. ARMED CONFLICT CRISIS

54 years of non-internationalized slow armed conflict between Indonesia and West Papua without foreign government attention. Why Indonesia is not signatory state of the Rome Statute of the International Criminal Court (RSICC), real consequence are humanitarian assistance and foreign interference for peaceful solution never delivered yet, hence Indonesia completely disobeyed International Law of Armed Conflict (ILOC) rules. Indonesia via foreign aid funds bought high technology equipped military tools including air craft, weaponry and warship to control the territory when West Papua's independence aspiration gained regional support 2013 and greater international community awareness.

A. SHORT HISTORICAL VIEW

The armed conflict began since the Dutch left after UN took over the country. In 1963, UNTEA transferred into Indonesia under US mediation. In 1961, a pro-independence group of the OPM has established a Republic State of West Papua but claimed their independence sovereignty mostly via non-violent struggle method and poor military resource against Indonesia.

First president of Indonesia announced a triple people command; one of them was *'Abolished the Dutch made a puppet state' of West Papua*, to sustain this goal they urgently set up a sustainable military operation called *Military Operation Region (Daerah Operasi Militer)*. As an outcome they had 32 years of military dictatorship leader of Suharto, Indonesia's second president introduced more than 12 operations unit been killed 100.000 native Papuan, the most dangerous operation was sweep operation I and II in 1978-1980s.

The character of armed conflict is truly **non-international armed conflict** but it has been not internationalized yet. A key impediment is that Indonesia is not an obligatory nation of the RSICC and other potential factors including inaccessibility of media, foreign diplomat, activist and researchers report result in weakness of civil mobilization and disrespect of rule of law. Human Rights Watch in Jakarta recognized as non-international armed conflict slowly occurred during the eight Indonesian soldiers been killed by WPNLA in 2013 within one week warfare. To gain world recognition it always is difficult on this slow standard of insurgency despite third party intervention is emerging like Afghanistan and Congo.

From 19 July to August 2014 rising up again a slow armed war in Lani Jaya District resulted in two Indonesia army and 4 police shot-dead. Indonesian army groups had fled after they got attacked back by the West Papuan National Liberation Army (WPNLA) led by Gen. Goliat Tabuni. As responded back were confirmed that six West Papuans liberation army have been killed, two churches and public facilities and some housing having been burnt down by Indonesian coalition troops according to national and local media news. As an outcome, thousand innocent civilian is under fear of military operation at present led them to sickness, hunger, and live in fear that they might be killed.

B. Combatant Groups, Operation Tactics and Their Capability

The classification of the core combatant groups are PIAG (Pro-Indonesian Armed Groups) versus PWPIAG (Pro- West Papuan Independence Armed Groups). The PIAG has various force units (mobile police, national army and police, special force) plus foreign military aid of global anti-terrorist unit of 88 detachments. While PWPIAG at least WPNLA, despite ICG and Indonesian Government assumed a new armed group of KNPB but there was no evidence seen it then internationally believed it definitely not armed identical group. Another armed party also were involved as unidentified Groups, this is still debatable, most of NGOs and West Papuan claimed that this group is part of the PIAG which has been involved in killing of Papuans, but also Indonesia and foreign government have different insight.

They have different scale of military capability both the numbers and the bases. Proportion of military personnel between the PIAG and PWPIAG has totally imbalanced and it is hard to calculate in details from each of units including their war equipment characteristics. Obviously the PIAG members roughly estimated over quarter of 200 million of entire population in Indonesia ranked as fourth biggest military state around the world. PIAG consists of seven regional military command and national police even all force unit expanded into (more than 25 regencies, hundreds districts and villages) occupying the Melanesian West Papuan territory. PWPIAG consists of seven military command around the region with low level of personnel and military equipment, each with command of over thousands personnel but there no indication foreign intervention for military aid.

The 54 years of silent armed conflict counted over thousand incident via various tactics by PIAG some examples namely; in 1967 with OperasiTumpas (obliteration operation) were 1,500 alleged dead in Ayamaru, Teminabuan and Inanuatan; Apr of 1969; Aerial bombing of Wissel Lake District of Paniai were 14,000 fled to the jungle and 2640 dead in 1980s; From the PWPIAG has not many tactics at least attacking directly to military based around the areas and it said over 300 incident like 8 Indonesia army soldiers were killed by PWPIAG under General GolliatTabuni.

Silent matter of armed conflict invisibly and visibly undeniably prevailed in the region, currently both the combatant groups publicly declared a guerrilla war, ABC news on 11 July 2013 said a rebel leader Danny Kogoya (before he poisoned-dead by Indonesia) by vows to keep fighting Indonesia despite amputated leg with his members 7000, the other region claimed over 10 thousands of six regional command all over the country.

In the operation field structurally, the PIAG consists of two main troops are organic and non-organic troops, the organic win is based in West Papua and non-organic is additional troops during the war operation term. The soldiers numbers for additional troops is almost over thousands, the central operation regions are located in the middle highland of Paniai and Wamena, Puncak Jaya, border areas, and also the southern coastal of Merauke, Northern Coastal and small Islands of Biak and Serui, Western part of Sorong and Manokwari. Tactically, PIAG using air attack, suicide attack and target attacks via three central based operations; firstly air force with special target in the higher mountain areas where the PWPAG is based; secondly the army was established to military camp in the strategic places such near the where the native people based and public demonstration; navy operation for the coastal areas to control the sea. The PWPIAG basically direct and indirect target attacks into where the PIAG bases.

Foreign military intervention was emerged in Indonesia after destroying foreign investment and killing foreigners with Bali bombing in 2003 by terrorist network of Alkaidah. USA and other 34 states back up military training and facilities for Indonesia and global anti-terrorist unit of 88 detachments aimed to protect foreign investment, population and combat the terrorist movement. In fact this global security plan was misconduct under national authority of Indonesia because of separatism sensitivity, capitalist, and terrorist network interest. A General Commander of **Kelik Walik** was shot-dead by Indonesian special force 2009 and in the same year of 2010 other General Commander of Paniai Region Command, **General Tadius Yogi** was killed during no war time. This two incidents became public critics that misconduct of 88 detachment unit which heavily funded by the USA, Australia, New Zealand, UK, China, Russia have been involved unnecessarily killing in many incidents.

Most credible Human Rights organisation stated the both combatant groups are fighting mostly near the American owned gold and copper mine of Freeport-McMoRan areas. Indonesian government claimed to American aid worker shortage by PWPIAG in 2002 with no evidence trial in the court. According to local credible and well-known activist, Jones Douw, he reported that the foreign company back up Indonesian army against the PWPIAG. A example in 2012 local people found the PIAG used foreign company owned helicopter shot dead a young General Commander Salmon Yogi, and burnt out their base by air strike and target attacking. For PWPIAG have no evidence of any foreign assistance although a little humour, an Australian citizen Ukrainian, his name called Little stopped at Brisbane International Airport who wanted to travel to Papua New Guinea was charged him 10 year prison due to claimed himself as a General Commander to help military training for WPNLA fight to against Indonesia army.

Slow armed conflict is never-ending until final day of independence. Current shooting in-2015 in Timika, many innocents were killed in their homeland by PAIG, shot dead one teenager and three of them were injured during the fund rising activity. It was a little crackdown between West Papuan and INP, a weapon crabbed by member of fund raisers who assumed TPN member according to news then INP who trained by Australia and New Zealand shot dead a man and injured other 3 man plus over 20s been jailed. Now new additional PIAG will be established into two Indonesian provinces by 2015-2016; second Indonesian regional police headquarter at the Bintuni district in West Papua province and Wamena district of Papua Province for Mako Brimop or Mobile Police, then West Papuan people had rejected these projects. By extra PIAG sign of how

Indonesia ready to make open war against not only combatant of PWPIAG but at whole West Papuan civilians. Leo Magay Yogii, a new General Commander from Paniai regional was also killed by Indonesia military during no war time in Nabire 2015. On 27 December 2015, PWPIAG did direct attack to the PIAG base been killed 3 mobile police, two heavily wounded, 11 weapons crabbed including bullet and as response PIAG attacked back shot dead 1 soldier of PWPIAG at Agimuga district in Puncak Jaya.

C. ZERO UN's CONSISTENCY

United Nations was ignored in the achievement for a world mandate for peace keeping force and ceasefire plan in 1960s. In fact the two UN bodies were UNTEA and UNSF that led Pakistan troops of 1000 did not monitor international referendum so acronym AFC in 1969. Because of this UNSF troops was removed in 20 February 1963 before the referendum, hence, both the UN mission was dysfunction due to cold war until today there is no UN agencies to monitor and protect civilians including dissemination the factual information and first hand data.

Poor UN monitoring and reporting including foreign government concerns, the hostilities data of the 54 year of silent non-international armed conflict only been distributed by human rights organizations, journalist and local social and faith based community groups in very poor scale. According to multiple resources, it is believed that over 600.000 of West Papuan civilian died from the 1963 until present time and a lot of local groups claimed that over hundred thousand were wounded in many incidents in many places. Several incidents in different location and time namely, Arfai operation in 1960s, Biak massacre in 1998, Paniai rebellion in 1971, Wamena in 1978 and other places around the region with many cases but poor of reporting and dissemination data information. In terms of capital destruction very high cost was lost, local people claimed that over 100 public and private utilities including civilian property lost but poor with statistical data about kinds of property to make sure this figure due to media limitation.

The lack of legal capacity and UN intention in the armed situation hardly defined who the violator of the war crime is, crime against humanity including most importantly is the protection for the civilian. Despite 76 states have remained to Indonesia on human rights matter in West Papua in regards to important of the implementation for 180 point of universal periodic review protocols in 2012, but IHRL accomplishment is still problematic. In 2013, a president of the OUNHCHR responded an offensive force against civilian and activists, international security resolution is zero made, people of West Papua ask for a common ceasefire agreement by peaceful manner does not work because of distrust amongst themselves, the conflict party due to political sovereignty sensitivity. Some weaknesses are less internationalized about this slow armed conflict; there was no reaction by world government and lack of law enforcement it very likely that the ILOAC is absolutely dysfunction to put into a real action.

D. AUSTRALIA AND NEW ZEALAND INTERVENTION

New Zealand's police training aid was 5.4 million in 2014 while up to 200 million dollars of Australia's aid funds given to Indonesia in 2014 two previous year was 16.50 million 2011-2012, the aid budget has been increasing dramatically. In 2013 the letter replayed by the Government of Australia to International Forum of West Papua in connection to UN Peace Keeping Force inquiry was absolutely doubtful. In a little good response by Australian government, they have been endorsing to Indonesia to become obligatory state of RSICC and ILOAC for guarantee humanitarian bound. There was no sign on how much Tony Abbot, Australian Prime Minister has engaged to Indonesia on that case after the end of Australia's seat at the UNSC 2014.

New Zealand now on the two years position at UNSC from 2015-2016 after Australia ended non-permanent position at the SC. New Zealand has seen good sign support on stopping slow armed conflict by its action to not support police training to Indonesia. It is a very wise if New Zealand sets up more holistic approach on sustainable security and peaceful during the two years for concentrating on their Pacific conflict territories. New Zealand Green Party and NGO/CSOs continues to demand to cuff of military ties and advocate the political status at UN. A very strong party is Green Party along together with other small party in there, growing enough political party in Australia is Green Party, Independence Party, Liberal Democratic Party and Socialist Party. Those small parties, pacific community groups and West Papuan genuinely demand New Zealand's presidential position of the UNSC to resolve this slow armed conflict. They could do in diplomatic way by backing up to the UN to assess the decolonisation status and urging UNSC to recommend a legal inquiry on the territorial status of West Papua.

AUS and NZ are two big nations in the pacific region and they have a strong historical record on maintaining peace and security around the world. What they both should do, they can make a joining force in the spirit of empowering the regional government for security and peace mission in their back yard region like West Papua. Majority population from both countries continuingly demand their government to stop slow armed conflict that lead to extinction of the native pacific community under Asian country of Indonesia. To create a better security of West Papuan people, for AUS and NZ has committed in funding military and police training to Indonesian national army and police, badly it has not been achieved yet due to Indonesian sustainable security force operation and brutality are never-ending and there is no way stop it. New government with new foreign policy but their diplomatic cable stable between Indonesia, AUS and NZ, currently on 3 March 2015 Foreign Minister of New Zealand agreed to renew their police training ties according to their bilateral statement with its counterpart Indonesian foreign minister. Previously NZ has a green sign to stop its police and defence ties; it has become very easy in changing their commitment just like wind blowing in the last minutes for their national interest.

RECOMMENDATIONS

1. United Nations Peace Keeping Force urgently needs to deploy into this slow armed war region for pacific settlement propose according to UN Charter.

2. Indonesia asked to sign RSICC to maintain ILOAC.

3. UN Humanitarian and UN Human Rights Agencies must establish in West Papua to control the situation and provide humanitarian assistance for effected civilians.

4. This ongoing slow armed conflict must be addressed into UN meeting for state member attention.

III.4. DECOLONISATION DEVELOPMENT

Decolonisation is a global political development agenda that was decelerated by state members after two bloody world war, namely the first and the second. Those nations who strongly committed to accomplish eradication of world colonialism plan under the world body auspice. This decolonisation provision is excellent political will then has a positive impact if it is achievable in our dirty world today. Reconstructing this bed global political structure today is crucially important to overcome the unnecessary third world war occurring who knows, granting political sovereignty rights for

NSGT at UN list and the territory wants to be independent state, abolish current procedure of referendum system but set up new structure could be fair unconditional recognition. If the unconditional recognition aspiration is approved by state member it can be used as a constructive legal instrument in achievement the world obligation, oppressed people and decolonized regions will be able to enjoy their freedom. West Papuan endeavour maintains the global provision for the eradication of world colonialism, the struggle for political independence is also a part of it.

Final process of decolonisation is referendum but it is old style not new, very much manipulation in the record in many countries experience, therefore, West Papuan Independence Sovereignty seeking for Indonesian and world government for full recognition because the referendum was totally manipulated by Indonesia's domestic procedure of consultation in the past. The colonialists and world government gives independence unconditionally or by direct independence recognition will be the new modern paradigm for maintaining inalienable rights and independence sovereignty rights for every territory. The world referendum mechanism sometime leads to potential conflict, 17 NSGT on the UN list have been waiting for many years; it is still unachievable affecting their life in the hands of colonial rule.

Historical experience became very significant point of view to remember and remind the past mistakes made by states even whoever is the political actor. Political distortion and sentiment will never end, it defeats international law and natural law, this normative idea of Papuan is always on fire about their independence struggle. Obviously since first decade to second decade of eradication of world colonialism West Papua territory been neglected by world government and colonialist to gain recognition for decolonisation status. Then implementation on 1514 resolution and UN's Charter on universal declaration of Human Rights in introducing into colonized territory definitely unattainable legal resolution. The rule of law enforcements misapplied, very weaker, violated and killed the law itself together with destruction for territory and murdering people.

The global structure today was unable to impose the government's endorsement and commitment on a better realization, then UN authority do have more power to monitor and encouragement for their weaker attainment, there might be no sanction. In the new era of third eradication program period 2011-2020 where the number of state members working are only 17 remaining countries or any non-self-governing territories with non-listed at 24 committee also it will see at the end of the eradication year.

The international law is absolutely understandable but why the world legal authority would not be measure for what categorized people or territory eligibility granting a decolonization status. By new world order what kind of international procedure or protocol is required and how it can be done if non-listed territory inquiry is unaccepted. For the status territory of West Papua basically lawful to gain decolonized status quo to receipt international legitimating. Then theoretically it explains severe fundamental criteria are political history, new-colonial policy, geographical and ethnical distinction, subjection and domination, natural and human resources are other considerable and principal factors accordance to international procedures. Those conditions are fulfilled fully to apply West Papua to be decolonised territory.

How to utilise within action plan framework to support the world mandate for granting independence for colonial and people and territories by justify manner and without procedural limitation in the globalisation and modernisation epoch.

Today in 21st century, traditional mechanism for decolonisation plan under the new world order must be to modernise. Our world is globalisation era, hence, global structure must be renew in order to enhance global justice, peace and security through a pivotal approach. The current global decolonisation rule will have much better achievement if state leaders abolished the complicated old plan; third decade eradication. Attainment of a full independent NSGT either on list or not on the list has equal opportunity the same as equal human being. Writer critically provides some strategic ideas to endorse new action framework for the world colonialism eradication plan:

- Current referendum process required unnecessary financial budget expenditure and costing people's life under administering power even severe NSGT failed in their referendum because of manipulative procedure and administering power's colonial attitudes.

- International principle of referendum titled 'one man one vote' was definitely ignored cultural and ethnical identity system as unilateral nation. Last world nations or indigenous nations were undermined by current world rule. External rights of self-determination must be granted without precondition; recognition as state nation must not need to go through the process of referendum. In the global colonial eradication plan importantly to recognise the external rights of self-determination to the worlds indigenous community groups and abolish the recovery rule in the UN system before reinscribing their decolonisation status.

- UN Decolonisation Committee needs to establish a sub-committee on NSGT to address colonial territories not on the list all over the world and identify NLM around the globe in the implementation of eradication of the world colonialism. Over hundreds of NLM proactively seeking their independence sovereignty. It asks to remind colonialists' government not to stigmatise them into criminalist, separatist and terrorist movement like Indonesia the WPNLM of OPM or ULMWP called separatist movement. If not accommodated this critical opinion the armed war and human rights violations, criminalities and terrosist never and will not ever stop until doomsday or forever, all international law instruments and UN system can be dysfunction and they will go to hell. This critical idea must be understand by global policy makers and government leaders who supporting the decolonisation process, once approved it will help to reduce armed conflict and human rights tension.

III.5. MDGS IMPLICATION

MDGs operation in West Papua is completely sophisticated matter in relation to political and security pressure. It is inquired to have a measurable analysis study to assess what the positively and negatively impact for West Papuan independence struggle through accessibility global development agencies and their global plan. In 2000, for the same year of international declaration on millennium goals, the special autonomy law was offered to the indigenous Papuan after 2 years fall of big military dictatorship president of Indonesia.

International government agreed to back up the Special Autonomy with big hope that MDGs will be well implemented for West Papuan wellbeing, which was totally an unrealistic dream. On one side the delivery system was unclear and awkward; it was a key measurement of the 14 years MDGs implementation which was never achieved to tackle out socio-economic disadvantage. In the fact, the failure to meet the MDGs target was widely debatable issue in relation to stakeholders effectives and commitment, accessibility and armed conflict outcome. Lack of reporting, research and book publication about the armed conflict influence to the MDGs practices is part of denial by all stakeholders. Writer would like to briefly describe based on current condition.

Goal 1: Eradicate of Extreme Poverty and Hunger by Half

Multiple resources stated 86 % of West Papuan is still living under poverty line, and huge level is increasing steadily, financial mismanagement, corruption with Indonesian administration and armed conflict are part of core barriers. The 50 % of 86 % was contributed by slow armed war, civilian fled to the bush and no water and food led to die. UN poverty summit 2015 is not complete for Indonesia need another century to come, in connection to West Papuan must have to manage by their own government can be helpful to tackle out this global good program.

Goal 2: Reduce Universal Primary Education

Newer figures from UNICEF found that secondary school enrolment in Papua province is only 60% compared to the Indonesian national average of 91%. From different source found under 50% compared to national figure, thousands children who were affected by clashes between TNI and TPN moved to jungle and others thousand living near the PNG and Indonesia border.

Goal 3: Gender Equality and Women Empowerment

The armed conflict led to an increase in women literacy rate, which is very higher rather than men, sexual violation, abduction, and rape in the region seriously affected in loss of women's lives and development. In 2002 women in two provinces of West Papua held the lowest literacy rate of all Indonesian provinces, with 67,5 per cent, versus 78,4 per cent of Papuan men and an 85,7 per cent country average for women). Reported by Churches and local human rights institutions highlighted most Papuan girls rape by Indonesian force during their military operation in many cases, fled to very remote and isolated villages then their attainment in school was zero, the girls in the central highland of the military operation areas, where half of native population live did not complete elementary school but the girls in the remote coastal areas they only completed elementary school. Women's participation in politics was 5 % both their involvement in West Papuan independence struggle and higher official position of Indonesian government, for example one third of the seats of the Papuans People's Council is reserved for women.

Goal 4: Reduction of Child Mortality

The lack of immunisation access into war places and other factors led to the child mortality which was a high figure. And also the government and international and national NGOs have no factual statistics data. Nevertheless, local NGOs and Churches believe over thousand numbers of dead in less than 5 years as real outcome of the armed conflict between insurgency groups and government force. Such malnutrition of children under the age of five in West Papua is also higher than the national average of Indonesia due to food crisis for mother and children in the jungle.

Goal 5: Reduction of Maternal Mortality

From the maternal mortality rate of 1,116 per 100,000 births which is the highest in Indonesia, assumed 60% killed by this silent armed conflict in the potential conflict places especially in the remote. It was caused by sexual abuse of torture and rape during a decade war after MDGs operation.

Goal 6: Combat HIV/AIDS, Malaria and other Diseases

About 68 % of HIV/AIDS infected the West Papuan civilian due to unsafe sex workers, and in most cases it is believed that Indonesian Soldiers who were affected with HIV AIDS spread out around villages in higher number within war affected places. In Papua, HIV/AIDS prevalence among the general population (15-49 years age group) is the highest in Indonesia with 2.5%. 68% of HIV infected people are indigenous Papuans. In a new dilemma, it was found that in less than 5 years, 18 cases were affected positive with AIDS in Jayapura, the capital city of Papua Province. Their mother transmitted in their body.

A previous survey in 2006 showed the use of condoms for commercial sex workers was only 14.1%. Papua province with 38,449 cases which was highest rate of malaria compared to other region. Papuan highlands areas had no medical services, population distrust colonial health structure and system and inaccessibility in case of emergency (people have to walk for hours in the mountain), lack of confidentiality and discrimination. National standard guidelines describing the level of care are not enforced and are not adjusted to local practices so that community primary health centres and village dispensaries are of a mediocre standard, lacking trained human resources to cover the needs.

Goal 7: Ensure Environmental Sustainability

West Papua is second largest tropical rainforest islands in the world, this rainforest gives livelihood for majority of native population, the illegal logging, palm oil plantation development and aerial bombing, attacking have destroyed this natural richness and livelihood. In 2006, 38.7% of households in West Papua were using non-piped protected drinking water, especially the fresh water pipe was damaged by armed conflict recently in Pania, Puncak Jaya, Wamena and it is assumed they put poison in the garden infected dire illness for local people.

Illegal logging was a potential problem into two West Papuan province of Indonesia including massive environment degradation due to multinational corporation presence. The rebel groups of PWPIAG is located almost near the mining areas protects their fresh environment and fertile land as their source of life opposing the PIAG and as the foreign military troops take control of their company, then both the combatant groups fighting with targeted attacks strategy destroyed endemic species and natural vegetation during the war period. There are no indication foreign nations back up the PWPIAG for natural resources benefit against PIAG.

Goal 8: Develop a Global Partnership for Development

The political sensitivity is undergoing, foreign humanitarian aid workers and international humanitarian organisation prohibited to entry into West Papua even International Development Agencies of UNDP, WHO, World Bank have faced a limitation, as a result no previous study was conducted by them to assess how important it is to implement the MDGs to the armed conflict effected native civilian, this targeted groups need more help with international development agencies independently. Indonesian authority does not accept to report out the human rights, humanitarian, and domestics' political matters related to West Papua by those aid groups. West Papuan people extremely ask foreign development partner and agencies to do better treatment since they did not trust Indonesian government; entire MNCs operating in the region have good partnership with Indonesian military rather than West Papuan NGOs and Customary Council.

MDGs and Armed Conflict Analysis in General

Some general conceptual analysis of how the armed conflict affects the 8 point of MDGs that will always be challenging to the human security and socio-economic development for fragile states based on factual report of UN. This analysis based on the research in the fragile states around the globe such African, Middle East and Asian countries.

Goal 1: Eradicate extreme poverty and hunger

Crisis slows the economic growth and often reverses gains made against poverty and hunger. Continuing absence of basic security and corresponding low levels of confidence among economic agents undermines development policy implementation. Deep macroeconomic challenges often include large budget deficits, high inflation and a high debt burden. The location and type of conflict affects MDG status and economic growth variably, sometimes affecting whole countries and economies, while other times affecting geographic pockets or particular social groups more directly. Thus, there may be positive MDG progress at the national level despite on-going conflict in some areas. Though rarely the immediate cause of conflict, poverty can be a factor in its escalation and continuation, particularly when coupled with severe horizontal inequality; and it is statistically a robust indicator of conflict risk.

Goal 2: Achieve universal primary education

Education is often interrupted during conflict. Schools may be closed or destroyed. There may be a shortage of qualified teachers, due to persecution, flight, enlistment in armed groups or due to non-payment of salaries. Children may be trapped at home due to fighting or lack of transportation; or they may be forced to flee or are enlisted into armed groups. Others may abandon school to work or to scavenge for food. Even when children remain in school during crisis, their ability to learn is often compromised by hunger. Community efforts during conflict often provide a basis for primary enrolment to rebound quickly once conflict ends. But this depends on the speed at which communities can rebuild homes, shelter and livelihoods, so that children are not needed to support these activities.

Goal 3: Promote gender equality and empower women

Women and children are disproportionately the victims of conflict. They constitute the majority in camps for refugees and are internally displaced. Sexual violence is often used as a weapon of intimidation. Women and girls are routinely recruited, coerced or kidnapped to fight or to support armed groups. Following crisis, widowed women must provide for their families. But war may also empower women, as they often move into leadership roles, including running businesses, overseeing farms and commanding armed groups. In general, women often take up roles and professions previously dominated by men. These gains in gender equality however are often reversed following the resolution of the crisis. But they can also be leveraged in the implementation of MDG related activities.

Goal 4: Reduce child mortality

Conflict leads to higher rates of death among children through illness, disease, lack of immunization, malnutrition and violence directed against children and women. This implies a higher relative level of vulnerability for children in post-conflict countries, all else being equal.

Goal 5: Improve maternal health

During conflict, the health of expectant mothers can suffer and their access to healthcare and professional facilities may be limited. Mothers suffer from hunger, disease, exposure, dehydration, trauma, displacement or forced migration, rape and other forms of violence. Health clinics and hospitals may be closed or destroyed, and those open may lack essential medicines, supplies, electricity, water and staff. Expectant mothers may not be able to get to clinics, or even to give birth in clean conditions with the assistance of a traditional mid-wife. Likewise, there are serious implications for maternal health in post conflict countries as well.

Goal 6: Combat HIV and AIDS, malaria and other diseases

Poor nutrition, exhaustion, stress, unsanitary conditions, forced migration and close confinement increase vulnerability to infectious diseases, including malaria and tuberculosis. With male combatants on the move and rape used as a weapon of war, armed conflict can lead to the spread of HIV and other diseases. Conflict disrupts access to basic tools of prevention, such as condoms. The pursuit of Goal 6 is likely to be additionally hampered by the war-induced breakdown of health systems. But in some cases, and counter-intuitively perhaps, conflict may also work to reduce the risk of HIV infection or slow its spread by minimizing mobility and social interaction, halting trade, closing borders and isolating areas of the country for several years.

Goal 7: Ensure environmental sustainability

Conflict destroys the environment. Fighting decimates forests and agricultural land, and poisons water sources. People forced to flee place further strain on the environment by cutting trees for shelter and fuel, clearings forests for new farmland and polluting their temporary habitats. Crisis often drives rural inhabitants to urban areas that are unable to adequately absorb their large numbers, thereby straining public services and increasing slum dwellings. During conflict, extraction and harvesting of valuable natural resources are often conducted with little regard for environmental impact. Neglect of oil pipelines and mines and their destruction by warring parties causes further damage to ecosystems and to environmental resources. After war, the challenge is to repair this damage and to 'unlearn' the environmentally unfriendly practices that are rampant during conflict.

Goal 8: Develop a global partnership for development

Conflict disrupts trade and investment, and often interrupts important development assistance. The continuing costs of the military even after a ceasefire or peace agreement drain national budgets, increase the size of debt and strain economies. Scarcity of human capacity exists side by side with collapsed labour markets.

IV. World Global Rule Implication

Indonesia plus State Members have agreed to move in a new era of global development rule to maintain series of international law and treaties after a bloody world war experience which was caused a huge human suffering and victims including materials destruction. The globalisation is a pivotal way to interact with the modern society and traditional society to set up a new common values and norms for international society life, forgetting the past experience move to new ideas and experience whatever good or bed. A big impact from the forgotten and forgiveness even receipt mercy and amnesty according to current global structure on the contrary it is absolutely effecting in the completion for the rule of law itself; it is a simple example of how global ethics underpin the law. Obviously, these state members deny and doubt the issue with eradication of world colonialism, international law of independence sovereignty rights is still unachievable even in the 21st century, most of foreign aid agreement put place the idea of non-interventionism. Naturally the law of independence sovereignty is generated and it is of free value in common sense oppose the non-intervention law is newly adopted only to retain the colonisation system; there is no neutral international law on it. Hence, non intervention policy must reinforce again in shaping particular affairs such people in the NSGT under the foreign or colonial domination be able to uphold their absolute rights, not pose by wrong international policy.

The model of current world global system is a new colonialism rule set up by state and private actors (economist) in spite of the scholars and activists have been working hard to change a new global justice system, their critical suggestion basically abolishing the old colonisation regime. The politics and democracy has to be changed with full respect of the law and respect global civil society participation, our world belongs to everyone not only the state members and MNCs, international policy making procedure at UNGA is necesserly to be improve, veto rights system must abolish to create new vote system at UNSC and World Bank if all international political community groups wander to build up stable global justice system. This simple idea would be of help to global equitable society and family nations of UN and its people in their interaction more robustly. This new form of global system to ensure their development especially powerless society, minority groups, poor nations, two groups of LWN is indigenous nations and colonised territory like West Papua.

Global development agenda would be unworkable before settling up the political case; it had become core weakness under global government authority. A critical inquiry how much the neutral world body of UN has been experiencing in endorsing Indonesia's commitment in terms of maintaining the UNGA 1514 resolution since West Papua became victim of ignorance under this resolution of granting independence for colonial countries. In the global regime, the third decade of eradication of world colonialism cannot be a symbolic term but it must be realistic term to deal it. International public critic raise of the current globalisation system is completely a new colonialism model ruled up by powerful states and private actor or more economist orientation. Critical solution that scholars and activists need working hard to change a new global justice system by abolishing the colonisation regime concept, UN system need to be modernised and manageable to enhance political development and create more opportunity to all colonial territories participation. UN must have more authority to control states member and UN agencies for example UN 24 Committee expand to the whole colonial territories both NSGT on the list and NSGT not on the list, UN must advocate to the NLM groups around the world for their political participation in order to maintain the rule of law.

West Papuan is part of minority world population; whether their rights of world citizen are respected or not then it necessity to speak up on how many a global fundamental programs are applied. Indonesia never has been implementing the global obligation to ensure the quality of life although a series of international agreement was signed but zero realization became true factual reality. For instance, in 2006, Indonesia became member states of UN Human Rights Council, after three years West Papuan freedom of speech and movement was confronted by state weapon. During the celebration of world indigenous day, Tepinus Tabuni was shot dead by Indonesia military in 2009 even in 2011 Third Papuan Congress 6 activists were jailed, 3 activist were killed and more 300 hundred was detained for one week, no rights of world citizen and international indigenous rights for internal self-determination just in the UN Policy Paper, hence, international fact finding team is needed from UN to monitor the ongoing situation. On other side, Indonesia is permanent member of 24 committee of General Assembly, however, when West Papua is seeking their decolonisation status Indonesia never opened their mouth and open the 24 committee door to accommodate this NSGT included in the agenda despite the some pacific countries are Vanuatu, Solomon Islands, Tonga, Nauru and Tuvalu rose.

Three major problems included in the human rights atrocities, democracy crisis and insecurity are inseparably continually causing this unsettle political unrest; this silent concern matter should reach intention globally, however, for Indonesia and its cronies unwillingly to seeking a new political improvement plan. For public opinion that conflict both the parties have their different political sentiment to be substantial contribution over that case but also international regime attitudes in one side. The international government persistently is inconsistent and weaker in their endorsement to the Indonesian authority for real action on these global development agenda of democracy, human rights, peace and security in this colonial territory. If West Papua is minority international society; their minority rights have to be protected through global regime under whatever colonial government law and international law. For further deeper study about global regime behaviour and global interest within political community groups (state actors and non-states actors) for this political unrest will be explained in the next chapter, there are some who respected the mutual benefit and some did not respect their mutual commitment in their activities and interactions.

The world government likely to support whatever Indonesian colonial policies have been introducing to the West Papuan; put more non-intervention within domestic affairs upon the territorial integrity and sovereignty. The ranges of rule includes special autonomy law, demilitarization law and provincial separation rule, transmigration, UP4B, note given any positive effect these program have not improved the lifestyle in human life aspects at all (moral and cultural values) even human security programs does not work to preserve war, conflict and genocide. According to global plan, the United Nations committee on human security committed to enhance human freedom and fulfilment is fundamental principles for human dignity unless political limitation then it can be apply in ensuring human safety for trouble country. It is found that bad record of the human rights and militarism to be international critics today, human rights groups and the world Human rights institution claimed over 500.000 West Papua civilians dead according to 2012 report, even more during 3 years until 2015 believed to be 600.000 dead. That figures dislike what Papuan's assumption because they expected to be over one millions in the past 54 years excluding the killings during Dutch time.

Democracy and good government are part of main agenda of MDGs proposed to the third world countries; in relation to people of West Papua that living under the colonial domination have to examine how much their implementation through United Nations Development Agencies collaboration with government of Indonesia to accomplish these development programs. The argumentation is national authority as key obstacles and the responsibility of the world government never provided a good reinforcement to Indonesian and indigenous West Papuan. On the other hand, the benefit of financial foreign aid to support democracy and good government projects indicated that it was corrupted by Indonesian political elites moreover malfunction of the UN prevention corruption committee and Indonesian corruption eradication committee to control the financial operation. UN corruption agency can be able to work there, if any impediment exist what the alternative tool to fix up in relation to economic development and to make progress better democracy in the conflict country. There is a solid gap; international political economy influences are more dominantly contributed amongst multiple stakeholders to manage this trouble country and its complexity of matter.

In the multiple studies clearly defined the development of globalization force has potentially created a double consequence for the people in the colonial territory in the third world country. It has seen the cause that political investment more often perfect deal between the foreign government and the administering state. West Papua has been facing serious challenges rather than creating incredible prospect in progressing all development aspects, then badly economic liberation or free market, terrorism network and black market easily access into remote villages in the land, the state actor could not take any preventive efforts. The foreign government and the state also play behind it; such Indonesia organs supporting the terrorist movement already have infiltrated against these West Papua freedom fighters, foreign workers and journalists. Indonesia formed a joint multiple power with the 88 detachment unit or anti-terrorist program on opposite the native people activities around the multinational corporation areas and also illegal mining area such early last year, the MNC's helicopter, the 88 detachment and Indonesian combined military and police brutally were attacked TPN/OPM members in Paniai caused 20 people confirmed dead, many houses burnt down and five thousands fled to the jungle. Sadly, international ceasefire does not operate for that horrible war even for any international red cross for humanitarian mission in the remote potential conflict areas so outcome the victim and violators unrecovered it out.

The millennium development goals is a global solution in improving national development programs to progress the quality life for marginalised people and vulnerable community within third world country include West Papuan should be prioritised. The UN's development agencies (WHO, UNDP, World Bank) was emerged in 2006 after 6 years declaration, their practices and policies whether it engages to the local needs and problems or not need a deeper study the reality. What the local needs there is the underneath civil society fully participate from the policy making level to implementation process and also advocate the complexity of disadvantages problems by using those good agencies to help find out further constructive solution, at least the root of case in the country must to be resolved. Statistical data stated that the highest poverty rate in Indonesia from two provinces in West Papua was 80% native population, 70% infacted HIV AIDS. This can be a strong critical study why the ranges of development program always been politicising not well implemented at all on the bottom level.

Negative attitude of international government on realization global peace and security mission for this trouble country, the ranges of civil society groups have traced in same views about global government failure. Unsettled political war between West Papua and Indonesia, the international governmental organisation does not care even though hugely increasing the intensity of disobedience definitely denied to international law on conflict resolution covenant. It is widely debated distress for the doubt of world interference dislikely the world government overcome to the many conflict countries (Palestine, Afghanistan, Tibet & South Sudan) in history, therefore, the peace based institution and educational institution have a good commitment to manage this political ideology war through mediation approach. The Indonesian Research Institute and West Papua Peace Network have been facilitating a Jakarta-Papua dialogue agenda while the two conflict parties have different concept of dialogue which is not accepted by each other; for the West Papuan need a third party mediation dialogue with believe that the issue is part of international matter in the contrary Indonesia believes only in the internal matter. The remarkable achievement for this peaceful initiative already gained a greater reaction and support, SBY have agreed about peaceful approach since some foreign government pushed him to have an open dialogue agenda that can be viable manner. But in his regime already has missed out no commitment anymore now under new regime of Jokowi has a little good sound for Jakarta-Papua dialogue.

The world global rules need to be clear and it is one of the considerable points after a decade of 21st century. A good suggestion that how to set up a manageable, meaningful and achievable international policy to the all groups of political society and it also how to minimise state member's competitiveness and its interest that always kick off some good world global rule itself. The modernisation of the old global system according to our contemporary world is to make sure equal rights within global political community groups including national liberation movement in front of the law, the law is the bible for everyone on it. External rights of self determination with current world system is not help much for many regions in many years, massive killing led to genocide on behalf of this policy. Independent sovereignty and independence sovereignty rights are twined policy that always confuse in the practise then it equally is asked to reform.

Chapter II

INTERNATIONAL POLITICAL ACTORS INTERFERENCE

The international political actors are dynamic and complex in their interactions, reactions and behaviours thus, it is very interesting to search in their attitudes in a deeper understanding. The classification for those actors comprise of international and regional government body, individual state nation, MNCs, foreign religious groups, international civil society organisation and other non-state actor. Their interaction in the political life of West Papuan basically unique and challenging in the context of West Papuan political independence aspiration in the two century.

I. INTERNATIONAL GOVERNMENT ATTITUDES

DYSFUNCTION OF UNITED NATIONS DUTY

The complexity of it though and its political belief distinctions definitely verify what the international government attitudes are, their motivation and sentiment amongst interested political community groups including UN itself is considered to drive the force factor. Their reaction is still stagnant not renewed despite new epoch had moved a decade of the 21st century; hence the behaviour of world government draws various criticism and suggestions from many practitioners.

1. Firstly, the scholars by their empirical study analysis highlighted the government reaction became paradox,

and then their key recommendation suggested with peace solution but still weakness their endorsement.

2. Secondly, the activists believe to have not reactive attitude, which needs to do more general public pressure for international government action.

3. Thirdly, the grassroots community protest against in regards to their government behaviour change.

4. Lastly, the government leaders more defensive sustain their national interest; hence international society gives mistrust for government diplomats reluctantly their unresponsive attitudes and irrespective ethics in the global political interaction.

International negative behaviour is derived from state members of UN's practices and experiences that shown how much their intention in accomplishing international policy and provision through global authority who agreed them. It is far away of their good wisdom, West Papua unpleasantly absent if make comparison to early potential conflict territories in relation to the UN' interference was a good world reputation although in some conflict regions given public distrust to the international government's direct reaction. As newly independent states of Timor Leste, South Sudan and Kosovo were overwhelmingly emerged their world government reaction upon advocacy and investigation even fact finding mission to discover the roots problem and its solution. It took long process for third party assistance even UN due to two reasons, they are the colonialist's political bureaucracy and global regime structure practically, nevertheless such world mandate under full responsibility of this world institution in realization for these agreed global provisions because it is not a rhetoric theory.

West Papua's core aspiration to the UN is their past political distortion needs to be assessed analytically the standards of its achievement had taken during the AFC of 1969. The UN failure in upholding its charter and provision unquestionably became legal dispute such as many historical books have explained deeply that political manipulation under national authority of Indonesia and UN auspice did not ensure international law obligation. Normatively, UN's main duty is duel the encouragement and monitoring state members' interaction in achievement of their world mandate, the UN capacity limitation to engage the colonial authority and its colonial system in the post second world war era was totally disobeyed in international political norms. The UN expert said a core impediment was removed by the Indonesian membership status from the state members of the UN, it is reasonable to cold war hegemony, that great momentum quickly set up their colonial strategies and policies for ongoing military operation and set up official government departments and building university and school in the territory for example paradise university in Jayapura, the capital city of Papuan province. UN lost power to intervene and monitor the country directly; hence, UN did nothing in the young age of 20 years although UN has given a world mandate takes full responsibility for control colonial territories and people. The UNTEA as UN mission into West Papua utterly was dysfunction to accomplish its responsibility. UNTEA did not recognise the West Papuan national symbols such as the Flag, Currency, Defence and Security under New York Agreement.

A call for international government interference has been the key aspiration since the failure of international referendum in 1969. Despite that the failure of one man one vote referendum was denied by colonial states within new world regime, nevertheless a wider assertion suggests a deeper clarification of the historical documents to further legal justification for the political history distortion widely remain today. The UN is the only neutral world body, there was no indication its neutrality values was practiced in the case of West Papua in some aspect. The UNGA on Fourth Committee of Special Political and Decolonization ought to identify the case and to implement the eradication of world colonialism provision to end a new global colonialism model threat to the colonial territory and people of West Papua. Global Civil Society Groups role was enough advanced to promote and convince a request for foreign government interference fairly and democratically. Current global structure gives a little space for civil society organisation participation, Pacific Conference of Churches continuation call to reinscribe West Papua into the C-24 during the Pacific Regional Seminar on Decolonisation from 21 to 13 May 2014 in Fiji. This call was trying to make a positive move in terms of international government behaviour in order to get more reactive attention on the case of political unrest.

Writer truly believes that only the vibrant global structure can be able to accommodate minority's political desire. It describes if state members design useful world mechanism and legal procedure especially set up proper advocacy and monitoring scheme will have direct impact to enhance the equal opportunity for politically disadvantage society groups within conflict region. The public distrust stressed with the current world order due to some limitations are UN representative offer into this region politically restricted, mutual distrust between the both governments, political manipulation all over the agreement made, their ineffectiveness and unaccountability publicly always be invisible.

The current structure of minority groups protection cannot guarantee their future, the national mechanism have to be equal to the global rule one or equal balance of structure is meaningful one and manageable for minority wants. NGOs/CSOs groups, government and NLM groups or whatever they are, have equal stand and position to determine their future position through global order. Political minority groups have to be free from any persecution by sovereign state authority either military neither police, today UPR rule need to put more workbale regulation on that areas. To enhance this

UPR should be introduced into a new spur procedure like establish UN body of minority groups. UN body to control separatist or independence movement groups is needed to respect international fundamental human rights law. West Papua Independence Groups is political minority groups within Indonesian rule. Why this group is part of minority: their independence sovereignty aspiration closed off under military power of Indonesia, never invite this groups into peaceful negotiation table, neglected their freedom of movement and association; ban their political activity during 54 years, mostly very poor condition on the land of Papua. Those qualities could be categorised into the minority condition never undermine by whatever colonial or whoever by narrow explanation.

The global government mechanism and structure barriers to be a key dimension on the standard of multilateral government attainment for global security and peace provision fulfilment in the trouble zone. It has seen under the new world order, their protocol and procedure on delivering those international covenants and resolutions was definitely impracticable because the trouble region within the poor or most corrupted states and bed domestic authority directly affect to the global peace and security in application scope. For nearly half of the century the native minority people have got psychological and moral suffer from their colonialist worst treatment, misinterpretation the minority and indigenous rights norms according to the benefit of national politics at all places, the special autonomy rule of West Papua is not guarantee to be joint into UN Indigenous Forum. The global authority does not help to undermine the national barriers, good collaboration existence between and in them not developed due to all the interested party controlling and stimulating each other just concentrate on their individual benefit. Then the question is the education of global structure and mechanism a central duty for general public understanding especially Indonesian nationalist in order to improve their future policy making process.

Indonesia has lack of education and awareness for global justice and democracy development.

UN General Secretary, Ban Ki Moon voywed his hand to West Papua Solidarity Group during PIF Meeting in Auckland, 2011

Multilateral international government reaction like United Nations on the pacific regional meeting became a good historical period of the West Papuan struggle in gaining international public attraction. The UN top leader, Ban Ki Moon remarked clear statement that the matter should be discussed at the decolonization committee after over 50 years never mentioned by previous UN leaders. A great diplomacy success was worked by 4 exiled leaders were Dr. John Ondoame, Rex Rumaikeik, Pauola Makabory and Amatus Douw who was collaboratively working with their support groups made a new advanced diplomacy in New Zealand. A wider critic traced the UN encouragement on regional human rights and democracy problem was not enough to give any positive influence in the behaviour change of regional government. A beneficial point might be taken into account, was pushed regional wisdom about the matters whether pacific leaders could take reaction or not if the global agenda introduced into regional authority. The third decade of eradication on world colonialism included several pacific territories within decolonization status except West Papua. Since world neutral body made clear picture for the political status of the trouble territories in the pacific region, therefore, West Papuan gain more confidence the case bring through the UN decolonization desk.

The world forum is the best impetus traditionally to rise up multiple potential matters around the globe. In spite of this, it has always faced critical process like forum procedure and protocols restriction for the world minority society groups for their inaccessibility to vote their political aspiration. After the world body of UN formation the territorial status has been raised without West Papuan attendance in 1960s, even the majority state members were not always interested in the issue whilst other interested states party play double role for their diplomatic interest with Indonesia. In the 21st century Vanuatu and Nauru ever been decelerated legally to support the independence struggle in the General Assembly meeting in 2000. Paradoxically it rose again in 2010 and 2011 with a little good conversation amongst the state member representative of South Africa, Papua New Guinea, New Zealand, Ireland, and Switzerland around the issue of the right to self- determination, Indonesia and their counterpart state like Afghanistan confronted but for others states absent according to wiki leaks source.

The 68th General Assembly in 2012, international public critics overwhelmingly remarked to Indonesia in relation to human rights matters in West Papua. More than 76 State Members and non-state members of NGOs raise a huge critics became real historical international protest momentum after 52 years of doubt. Their strong recommendation has passed was a peaceful dialogue and effective implementation for the 180 point of UPR to maintain human rights law in West Papua; nonetheless, their action was weaker to influence Indonesian behaviour in one case. The commitment of Vanuatu government radically existed to seek an UN initiative, after two years, Prime Minister Moana did a strong speech to acknowledge UN and government leaders in regards to human rights impact on West Papua in 2014. In here not arguing on voting rights system but how to use UN authority pushes Indonesia.

Did UN control the effectiveness on all the international treaties in Indonesia? Two reasons, firstly UN endorsement itself was very slow and Indonesian authority prohibit the entry of UN Body into the region. Why Indonesia fear to not signature and ratified yet the Rome Status of International Criminal Court. When Indonesia absent of the ratification on international treaties does not mean that UN could not monitor these but UN has duty to bear these. A big nation had recognised the long enduring armed conflict; the letter dated on 29 April 2013 to International Forum for West Papua that Australia had recommended Indonesia in 2012 during the UN meeting for UPR to ratify the RSICC. It was very principled and meaningful one for their main theme at the UNGA meeting in 2012 was *"judgment and settlement on international disputes by peace means"*. RSICC treaty qualifies the eligibility with slow armed war between TNI and TPN, crime against humanity and terrorist widespread in West Papua territory. What the criteria and procedure to use in term of UN reinforce Indonesian, use of UN authority for human security and peace commonly acceptable ethics, therefore, now whether UN ready or not, it is a rationale question mark.

UN in the 21st century has paved a little attention to West Papua in human rights and political case. Two UN special reporters (Mrs Hina Jilani & Dr Manfret Noak) on their report expressed that *the climate of fear undeniably prevails in West Papua and the torture and rape became daily basis based on their visit in 2008 and 2007*, good report and recommendation had passed but without further action by UN authority. Ban Ki Moon, UN leader has different view of the West Papua case with Timor Leste. In his visit in 2012 his comments on the media that Timor Leste was not part of former Dutch colony dislike West Papua. But U.N. genocide expert Mendez reported some concerned countries including those of Northern Uganda, Myanmar, West Papua in Indonesia, Central Asia and the Caucuses and Colombia categorised those indigenous populations are at risk of extinction. UNHCHR, President 2013 remained to Indonesia to stop repressive action for civilian in West Papua. All the UN leaders and Officials have paid very little attention in the 21 century, former UNSG Kofi Anan agreed to establish Inquiry Committee for West Papua with Deputy Prime Minister of Vanuatu in 2004. Even Kofi Anan himself was against the result of AFC in 1969 when He became a young diplomat from Ghana during UNGA debate, He understood well about political manipulation of territory but missed his 2 terms of the UN leadership, which was 8 years. Furthermore former UNSG, Uthan from Burma during the cold war era. He lacked leadership capacity on West Papua which might be because of his Asian background. He fully focused on Asian countries under the UN authority attention.

In the world's view that pacific countries are small and minority in regarding to sharing global power for our world. Regionalism issue in the new world order system is there, regional division power for world leadership is there, now coming to question that why from time to time the leadership of UN from the other part of the region is not from Black Oceania or Pacific Region. Regional block sovereignty should be recognised and it must threaten equal order. Diplomatic and resources weakness cannot be key barriers because as the independent sovereign states have shared equal power and responsibility for our world. Pacific Islanders Countries must fight in order to gain the UN leadership role at least UNSG, many cases in our region never been top agenda of UN, from the political matter to environmental. Pacific region countries, peoples and territories are sometime ignored by UN authority; other regions are very dominant in the UN system. If Pacific people take control UN authority especially UN secretary, President of UNGA, President of ICJ will be create better opportunity to address political and legal matters in our region so that political status of West Papua can be resolved through UN mechanism.

Is West Papua located in Pluto planet or our Earth planet? Armed war between TNI and TPN is enduring in the eye of UN and world government over half century. What five veto powers at UN Security Council include USA, England, France, Russia and China have concerned on that particular armed conflict territory. All veto states have a very strong link to Indonesia. The Security Council is the machinery body of UN to control the war and to bring peace and stability. UNSF and UNTEA ever have operated in there not maximal to fix out the territorial status, out of international rule and world obligation, hence, both the UN institution urgently needed to be reactivate again. Aspiration of West Papuan people is resolving the problem through international order or UN auspice because they definitely believe that the root case for the political unrest and human rights atrocities will be ended through it.

II. REGIONAL GOVERNMENT GROUPS

The West Papua case was very low degree in the standard of regional governmental groups' reaction for almost 53 years. Seeking a regional intention and endorsement by the regional leaders have no choice to help their minority people, it is to gain regional recognition upon seeking regional solution to solving out this political turbulence. The obstacle factor is inconsistent with their constitutional principles and values for all the regional governmental groups within six continents in the world (PIF, AU, EU and ASEAN) completely lack of regional wisdom and moral responsibility. There was very little attention from the regional governmental organisations on the matter of human rights abuse unless they recognised rights of self-determination and independence aspiration.

II.1. MELANESIAN SPEARHEAD GROUPS

Melanesian Spearhead Groups is a sub-regional governmental group consisting of 4 independent nations and one non-self-governing country of FLKNS. This regional body aimed to fight together to end the colonialism in the Melanesia territories and to gain full political sovereignty rights of independence equally to other independent states in the Pacific Rim. They do step by step political plan to resolve up the conflict, a major program is to support these colonial Melanesian territories through decolonization desk at UN and it also grants the territory for full member like FLKNS then West Papua to be next target territory for full member in term of seeking decolonization status as NSGT at the 24 committee. It will be become very successful for MSG's political program if West Papua was accepted as full member in the future.

Seeking a full membership into MSG became a long ongoing controversial matter amongst all political community groups, it has caused very dynamic interests, both internal and external party of MSG was involved 3 years. Some reasons are, they are smaller and poor states to develop their program effectively. Three of MSG state members have strong economic ties with Indonesia, outside party influences and less commitment by MSG leaders to finalize their political provision.

A decade after the 21 century the MSG has a little attraction; 20 years Melanesia people and Vanuatu stand up as they feel more confident to engage with one of very sensitive matter of West Papua. The situation became higher risk for their Melanesian people and a little world community concerns on ongoing human right abuses as well as good diplomatic work of West Papuan in every single moment and even upon regional forum. UN key leader, Ban Ki Moon reminds them through media language that if the regional leaders or regional governmental body bring the case to the UN, UN can work as recommendation or mandate given by them. This historical remark is how important of regional leader and government must to have a good faith to resettle out it.

However, sub-regional government gives a little intention to West Papuan demand of observer status has been accepted by ministerial council of MSG. Although it gained a little attraction regionally and internationally, it will see for real action of UN & MSG how both the government can put the West Papua into third decade of world colonialism program or not depend on political development.

Extraordinary diplomacy winning at subregional government level, the MSG leaders has agreed to uphold inalienable rights to self-determination of West Papua 2013 in Noumea. But WPNCL application for full membership was ignored by MSG leaders excluding Vanuatu, asked more representative and fresh application. Vanuatu had facilitated West Papua Leader meeting 2014 December formed ULMWP and logged application directly to MSG Secretariat Office on 4 February 2015. In 11 February 2015, Vanuatu Official made statement to support full membership application in the next MSG meeting will held in Honiara, Solomon Island in July. ULMWP SG travelling around to meet the MSG government. There are two MSG leaders who strongly support permanent membership application namely Prime Minister of Vanuatu, Hon. John Natumen including Chairman of MSG and Spokesperson of FKLNS, Victor Tutugoro. Prime Minister of Papua New Guinea, Hon. Piter O'Neil also stated on the media to support the application because the human rights violation was threaten by Indonesian force while Prime Minster of Fiji and Solomon Islands have no sign whether they can support or not. It was very sure the membership application of ULMWP will be accepted by the MSG leaders at the meeting in Solomon Island on June 2015. If West Papua territory regains a full membership at MSG, it will have more opportunity for regional and international lobby and advocacy, the next step is seeking the other Polynesian and Micronesian of the PIF support before bring to the 24 committee of UN Decolonisation.

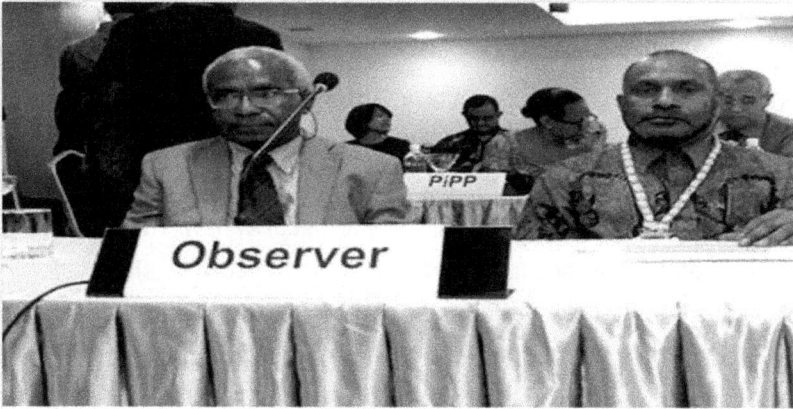

Octo Mote and Benny Wenda at MSG after gained Observer Status

Final decision by MSG leaders was less than what West Papuan appealed for it. Full membership inquiry was manipulated by Indonesian money politics to shut off the mouth of three Melanesian Prime Ministers; they were Piter O'Neil, Frank Bainimarama and Sato Kilman except Menase Sogavere from Solomon Islands. A miracle solution came out in the final communiqué that ULMWP agreed to give an *observer status* and Indonesia granted to associate member, it is equal position on the MSG forum. Melanesian states acknowledgment and recognition on West Papuan independence struggle is very essential, the world government and community always watching, this was a historical one after many years left them alone to struggle. Key reason the ULMWP presented in the regional forum for political aspiration and independence through international mechanism, MSG government authority put back West Papua in UN Decolonisation list. Indonesia was unhappy in one aspect but another aspect it had a big smile; they have more room for closer engagement with MSG in order to block what West Papuan political independence aspiration.

II.2. PACIFIC ISLANDS FORUM

The PIF is regional governmental institution that comprises of Melanesia, Polynesia and Micronesia countries and territories aimed to share the common interests and activities for positive benefit of native pacific people. In social and security law, their excellent policy for human security is reducing and resolving all conflict in peaceful manner. As basic resolution in the critical situation, Slade 2011 identifies severe methods of third party mediation, fact finding mission and regional dialogue by appropriate mechanism that would assist a resolution, within 50 years this regional policy did not work in engaging the West Papua's case, it became international public acknowledgement.   Seeking regional identity to the members is hopeless at the end.

Pacific native groups continuingly inquire to full participation in annual meeting for policy making purpose for their pacific lost territory of West Papua. As South Pacific Commission (SPC) is partner member at PIF, West Papua was active member at the SPC but now both PIF and SPC are not members. While Indonesia as post forum dialogue partner at PIF have faced difficulty to get membership status for West Papua because Pacific plan no support offered to West Papuan Independence Movement (Murray, 2011). PIF's ignorance of this regional minority society group of West Papua in the 21st century began in the 33th of PIF meeting on 15-17 August 2002 in Suva Fiji since then forum leader welcomed the special autonomy law of Papua under Indonesian rule. They wrongly believe that through this law, they will stop the long ongoing violence stopped by peace means and human rights values will be ensured. In 2006, on the 37th of PIF held again in the same country in Fiji, Forum leader welcomed Indonesian established Papuan People Assembly (PPA) to represent West Papuan people at PIF and call again all conflict party who contributed in violence to seek peaceful ways which was stipulated on their Leader Communiqué. One of good response by PIF leaders urged to Indonesian authority brings all perpetrators of serious crime into justice court. Therefore, PIF gives financial assistance for special autonomy development program activities and Indonesia failed to develop better life of West Papuan in the real field.

The negative regional behaviour of Pacific Island Forum is one good example of ignorance in maintaining their regional identity values as their pacific indigenous population; it has drawn critical inquiry for the reason of long term never had been regionalizing the agenda of West Papua into PIF plans. The big worry of losing a historical and anthropological kinship is remarked by underneath society groups continuously to ask legal authority to uphold ethnical development for this pacific native people who are imposed by Asian state of Indonesia.

Despite UN Secretary General, Ban Ki Moon on his media statement that West Papua issue should be discussed on 24 committee but pacific regional leader never been replied in PIF Forum 2011. Inconsistency of International & regional governmental groupings to deliver the political agenda faced public distrust, they are not good leaders in our planet. International human rights lawyer groups asked how much UN authority itself to approach on armed conflict in the region. Jenifer, a Australian International Human Rights Lawyer stated on her article that Ban Ki Moon efforts was slow after Indonesia pressure to not comment or raise the political status of West Papua case at UN forum or on behalf of UN secretariat authority.

PNG is a respected regional leader for PIF in 2015. On 9 February 2015, Prime Minister Peter O'Neil spoke out military operation in West Papua that was never the concern of the previous country leader; PNG wants to encourage regional government and individual nations. PNG by his good attitude was appreciated widely by Vanuatu Government and Australian Lawyer, Pacific Solidarity Groups and many others. Lowy International Policy Institute analysed that O' Neil avoid any direct statement on West Papuan independence aspiration and full membership Application for MSG. Although it does not mention on separatist movement but PNG Foreign Minister addressed his Government position on recognising West Papua is part of Indonesia after wider unclear statement on the social media. Given below is the original speech: *Papua New Guinea today is a respected regional leader. After 40 years of undisturbed democracy, we are in a unique position to lead mature discussions on issues affecting our people in the region. Our leading role in encouraging Fiji to return to a democratically elected government and voicing our concerns about the plight of our people in New Caledonia are examples of our growing influence. We have also participated in the restoration of democracy and law and order in countries like Vanuatu and Solomon Islands. But sometimes we forgot our family, our brothers and sisters, especially those in West Papua. I think as a country the time has come for us to speak about oppression our people. Pictures of brutality of our people appear daily on social media and yet we take no notice. We have the moral obligation to speak for those who are not allowed to talk. We must be the eyes for those who are blindfolded. Again, Papua New Guinea, as a regional leader, we must lead these discussions with our friends in a mature and engaging manner.*

In the regional leadership role, it has shown Australian supportive behaviour for PNG stand and other country more confidence his regional leadership in relevancy with population, resources, growth, border land and West Papua uprising. Now time has come to gain more power from other MSG countries, of course Vanuatu will stand if PNG was proven as a real supporter for West Papua course at the regional level, Australia can be first target to put pressure might be heard on. Another regional leader country is New Zealand who has a strong reputation in enhancing regional peace and security, former Prime Minister and Foreign Minister has asked the Indonesian president for dialogue, even today government has shown a good sign.

New history began after the Sub-regional committee successfully passed the West Papua issue as one of five priority agenda during the PIF leaders' summit in PNG 7-12 on September 2015. General Secretary of PIF made strong words for West Papua's vital contribution from the past relationship to PIF. Taylor explained more significant connection to the political, cultural and historical links that why leaders cannot make right decision on West Papua case. CSOs with PIANGO have strongly pushed back West Papua into Pacific family, Emele Duituturaga Director of PIANGO, political analyst and media highlighted there was only two top agenda that will be discussed on Leaders' Summit, that agenda on media everyday were climate change and West Papua locally, nationally and internationally. Secretary General of PIF, Meg Taylor stated three key recommendations namely fact finding mission, reinscribe West Papua to Decolonisation and give sanction for mining corporation who were involved in human rights violation.

Pacific leaders have very different view in the case of West Papua, Prime Minister of Solomon Islands standing position was very strong, he saw very strong leadership to back up with three agenda while Prime Minister John Key wandered to deal with Indonesia for fact finding mission and He willed his country to fund on this fact finding mission plan if Indonesia allow them to West Papua, Prime Minister Piter O'Neil have similar though with Key even other leaders. Indonesian vice foreign minister has rejected the fact finding mission, pacific leader initiative against non-intervention international treaty and recognise their national human rights commission that doing right job, however, Sogavere responded defensively in which distrust Indonesia human rights authority and as a state leader motivated to maintain the human rights law of self-determination and independence. The leaders have a critical and constructive discussion at all levels, the final communiqué from the three points, only one succeeded; regional leader agreed to send fact finding mission in the end of their long debate.

Two constructive resolutions came out on dealing the human rights problem in the pacific respected territory. Here is the original leader's communiqué has stipulated on their official website:

West Papua (Papua)

16. Leaders recalled their decisions and concerns expressed at their meeting in 2006 about reports of violence in Papua, in which they also called on all parties to protect and uphold the human rights of all residents in Papua and to work to address the root causes of such conflicts by peaceful means.

17. Leaders recognised Indonesia's sovereignty over the Papuan provinces but noted concerns about the human rights situation, calling on all parties to protect and uphold the human rights of all residents in Papua. Leaders requested the Forum Chair to convey the views of the Forum to the Indonesian Government, and to consult on a fact finding mission to discuss the situation in Papua with the parties involved.

Regional leaders' commitment and attitudes will examine their pacific society groups and West Papuan people through ULMWP based on how much they have done it. Implementation on their fact finding mission plan and how they can find other solution depends on them, Pacific NGOs groups, people and West Papuan is not enough accept for this agenda, more confident for them with forum observer membership and bring back to decolonisation desk. If Indonesia rejected and or agreed for this fact finding mission what will happen, it is a very essential question to be raised. What West Papuan reaction can take up for next step and how to deal it, writer provides personal opinion that some strategic points need to be done.

- Firstly, endorse PIF leader to involve independent experts, media and pacific senior politician as part of regional fact finding mission team.
- Submit a proposal on West Papuan view that refers what key party is important to meet them such as civil society groups, religious groups and independence groups into both Indonesian provinces, West Papua and Papua.

Many others can add to the points above in terms of the time of reference and the code of conduct for this regional fact finding mission.

II.3. EUROPEAN UNION

European Union is a powerful IGO regional bases which consists of colonialist countries in the political atmosphere. One of the EU goals was motivated to assist their former colonial countries in various ways and divers ambition in international political life today. West Papua is a former Dutch colony. International resolution has passed through UN to give former Dutch Indian territories for independence after EU nation ratified UN charter, treaties and provision. Netherland government promoted social economy development in West Papua since recolonised by Indonesia. After entry into the 21st century, the new Indonesian colonisation policies of special autonomy was recognised by EU state members, the first regional governmental body to do so and are main donors for special autonomy funds. In 2007 and 2008, fours EU nations visited into region to assess the implementation of the special autonomy; they found no improvement then urged Indonesia for more effective and serious in its implementation, these four countries of Germany, Portugal, Norway and Ireland continuingly funding in the name foreign aid project. They also point out some barriers that the special autonomy was rejected by West Papuan, gradually increasing human rights violation record and marginalisation leading to poverty and genocide. EU disrespects on the West Papuan political aspiration for independence oppositely West Papuan disrespects EU foreign policy for their cooperation with Indonesia in term of investment and trade. EU own attitudes toward West Papuan self-determination and independence plea desperately deft and blind to help out from their neo-colonialism stand.

Some EU parliament made robust encouragement. This request was directed to the EU foreign minister affairs to continue it to push against their unworkable bureaucratic attitudes in the past. On 26 March 2014 in Brussels they have passed a motion wherein the 16 EU parliament members signed several important recommendations to call: peaceful resolution by dialogue between West Papua and Jakarta; free access media, EU observer, UN Human Rights mechanism, support legal reform to ensure independent military court system for their act against civilian accordingly UN norms; Armed delivery by EU states not to kill native Papuans. Since that year SBY met his counterpart partner Queen Elisabeth in 2014 just to discuss the LNG tangguh project owned by British because this company is controlled by military force. One of the urgent appeals upon motion is to ban unjudicial murder by using EU imported weapon for Indonesia; however, on 8 December 2014 were killed four Papuan students and others wounded in Paniai, it was real example. What was EU reaction on it, this mass killing which has happened indicated arm trade, which is EU countries have strong military aid to Indonesia.

EU government leaders must learn from this experience, they need to give distrust for the Indonesian military court system, cut off their military aid and arm trade if EU willing to ensure mass murder not going to be happens again in West Papua, and also ensure a peaceful demonstration asking for internationally mediated dialogue.

European Union ambassador engagement with regional issue was historically sound in order to more actively encourage the Pacific leaders in their policy making process and take a real action for problem solving on those challenges and barriers in the lives of native pacific community. *European Union Ambassador for the Pacific, Andrew Jacobs, opened the forum, reiterating, "The European Union is proud to support this initiative. Promoting a strong voice for civil society and effective dialogue with leaders will result in more inclusive and effective development and benefit the people of the Pacific."*

EU Ambassador also recognised on three fundamental recommendations on the West Papua's affairs was submitted by NGOs Groups and PIF secretariat, a critical question whether he will bring in this particular case to EU leaders attention or not. Writer also look at how important it is to build up their cross party relationship between two regional block of PIF and EU in order to agree collective action in key regional agenda especially West Papua case. Both the body has a strong historical ties and good partner in international matters, pacific territories and independent nations were their former European colonial countries and European popular culture like Christianity.

II.4. AFRICAN UNION & ASEAN

African Union and ASEAN are two racially radical regional blocks on the earth, two blocks is most important actor might contribute into conflict between Indonesia and West Papuan. Some rational ideas that Indonesia is Asian race, West Papuan are black race, if they do assessment their involvement from anthropological approach. ASEAN Development Bank mandated by General Assembly of UN provides social security for economic development was nothing in the outcome. ABD belongs to Asian people, territories; countries and does not belong to pacific people. Racial discrimination is always in practise in their bureaucracy system, when Indonesia wants to be leader of ABD all the money projects does not go through UNDP. ASEAN is never concerned about human rights abuses and democracy especially to this conflict territory of West Papua, ASEAN and ABD together dictated by Indonesia. While AU has been facing difficulty to look at West Papua's case, because they can only concentrate on their ongoing internal or civil war, this capacity does not have enough help to West Papua, however, some AU members have good insight for West Papua when it debated on the UN forum level.

It is very crucial to discover regional wisdom for restoring their past assistance and some similarities from their colonisation history, human race and experience. Several AU members against the UN resolution 2405, 15 African counties did not sign that resolution, which include South Africa, Senegal, Ghana and few others. OPM has established in Dakar capital city of Senegal in 1960s. It must be mobilising their stand for example discuses again on AU meeting. Some West Papua politician visited there for seeking regional attention, African countries have big heart to look after freedom cry by West Papuan. Even they advised that firstly gain pacific regional block support and we will back up later. Their promise offer themselves now after emerging regional concern that West Papuan desires to join into sub-regional body and MSG resolution 2013 to maintain West Papua inalienable rights.

Some solidarity groups from Academics and activist working promote the case of West Papua in the severe Asian countries such as China, South Korea, Singapore and India. Indonesia is the capital city country of ASEAN. In the history no one Asian nation has been against the UN resolution of 2504, Asian Development Bank takes over the world mandate on the economic development collaboratively working with UNDP in Irian Jaya. The active member of ADB is Indonesia, other members fully respect their traditional way to maintain their ties by not asking how far Indonesian treatment on West Papua. In the conclusion, both ASEAN and ABD, two regional institutions radically support what Indonesian want for West Papua territory, both the body radical and racial institution on this planet.

III. STATE MEMBERS ATTITUDES

The states actor will be described distinctly based on their interests and involvement. It comprises of colonial states, capitalist states, communist and socialist states, incredibly exercise their behaviour threaten to the West Papuan people. The classifications of colonial states are:

1. Those countries who are involved directly in political manipulation and annexation on the political status on West Papua namely Indonesian, United Kingdom of Netherland, Indonesia, and United State, Australia, UK and France.

2. Communist and Socialist are Soviet Union and China who backed up Indonesia to control independence movement.

3. Some capitalist states are Japan, Germany, and Norway.

Bilateral and multilateral ties in and between those countries with Indonesia overwhelmingly marked. The two power of communist and capitalist block competitively established their hegemony by taking control of this beautiful country like beautiful virgin girls sold out to Asian colonial states of Indonesia from the hand of European colonial nation of Netherland through US's mediation. This became fundamental utopia in gain those states support for West Papuan's political independence aspiration.

To clearly understand concisely will classify the different roles of the state actors. It has seen their competitiveness, attitudes, multiple interests and their future expectation to this rich territory and strategic conflict zone. Two major groups, namely the colonialist states groups and non- colonialist states groups, have different motivation and attitudes contributed to develop their competition for the benefit of the natural resources and conflict, most powerful player is colonialist states in politics, economic, security aspect rather than non-colonialist states. Colonialist states (The US, Dutch, United Kingdom, Australia, Russia) behaviour more predominantly play double role in various ways. Moral obligation was denied to ensure their responsibility for world obligation accomplishment such as the Dutch did not restore his promise given independance while the US took over UN duty, it was organized a genuine referendum through a *New York agreement*.

When the Capitalism, Communism, Terrorism, Christianity, Muslimism became potential factor instruments into West Papua's life, it negatively impacted the native people's future destiny who being looking for their political independence sovereignty and true national identity. Capitalist and colonialist states groups aimed to maintain 95 % Christianity against Muslim influence and counter terrorism from West Papua, 2% Muslim has also expanded their business sector and control Christianity. Moreover Indonesia in cooperation with Russia and China expanded their communist and socialist hegemony with the goal to counter separatist movement and capitalist one. West Papuan lost originality and neutrality though, to determine their future nation destiny, due to all of the above hegemony has been radicals in young Papuan generation, and then no one is the best country or protector or respects the human rights norms in this planet. This foreign domination is the key weapon to destroy West Papua original characters and ways of thinking, belief and its act. Their behaviour motivated by their ideological hegemony, war between Capitalism and Communism, socialism, war between Muslim and Christianity, they empowered West Papuan as front liner in depending their ideology, they want West Papuan becomes fighter or warrior for their ideology war.

The above explanation came to reality today; Capitalist and Christian nations are dominant state party in relation to West Papua Territory, 95% West Papuan are Christianity followers. The world is led by Christian nations, from the government sector to private likely good sound for stand on minority West Papuan Christianity rights in Indonesia; however, they forget to look after this marginalised community. In some ways, Indonesian Church entities are controlling this minority of West Papuan; government funding more money at least to Indonesian owned Churches groups' rather than West Papuan owned Churches is being discriminated.

Foreign aid from government sector, private sector or international humanitarian organisations not going through the Church Channel should go through it for better service of the native people. Dr Benny Giyai leading Church of KINGMI Papua and Sofyan Yoman from Baptist Church only two grassroots community churches in West Papua, who are standing on behalf of their Christian people in the land of Melanesia, lack of financial resources not like Catholic Church. According to Indonesian government both the Church is labelled as separatist, they are living under persecution, their members, followers and staff targeted of persecution under Indonesia, many of them were killed and jailed. Christian nations never have been given any special attention despite West Papuan Church leaders have been crying for foreign attention. Church and Christianity came from Western countries spreading their Gospel values, Christian nations maintain their religious ideology for example fighting against Islamic State everywhere in our earth, Indonesia is Islamic state identically terrorist state colonising this 95 % Christian territory of Melanesian however, Australia, UK, Netherland and USA never fight them to defeat Indonesia from the land of West Papua. Communist and Muslim influence has been growing underneath society, just in a decade many West Papuan people can change their belief system and changed their faith to be Muslim and Communist or socialists. Negative impact is very sadly Native Papuan community will lose their original believe system.

III. 1. NETHERLANDS

Netherland became the first colony of West Papua territory; it was called Dutch New Guinea. The Netherland government's behaviour even in the 21st century has promised of giving independence for the territory is dead word. Dutch transferred the territory into his ex-colony country of Indonesia; obviously it seems like Dutch throws out West Papuan into the hell state, destructive situation such as murdering and genocide out of Netherlands governments' reaction. Nearly a million people died under Indonesian gun for 54 years, it has nothing to do with Dutch moral responsibility. The 21st century age, West Papuan entered into second generation living in Netherlands, thousands of West Papuan statesman were exiled there, many of them died in hopeless and ill full situation. They became voiceless and outside of Netherland government attention.

Netherland had promised to given independence for West Papua but long term denied their empty promise. It was measurable in 2004 since Netherland parliament passed an amendment to validate again the awful act of free choice; therefore, a Dutch historian Professor Dooglover wrote a book about West Papua's political history. In his book, he encouraged Netherland Government to pay moral obligation and say apology for past mistakes, for their denial in maintaining international law upon West Papua territory. Only few parliament members have willingness to back up the political status of West Papua territory after entering into the 21st century.

With regards to decolonisation status, Netherland is administering power and Indonesia only occupying power legally; decolonisation process is still open so Netherland government must put the West Papua territory re-inscribe at the 24 committee. Legal inquiry on the territorial status for West Papua under UN and Netherland Government authority principally meaningful ways, Netherland need to be big heart for West Papua to open the case through international mechanism. West Papua itself has been working on that approach together with Vanuatu government, West Papua Decolonisation Committee and International Lawyer groups of ILWP. By 2015 gain enough confidence for the ULMWP with observer status at MSG to more effectively mobilise resources and state members support before take real action to the world court.

III.2. USA & RUSSIA

During the two powerful states cold war era, America became winner. Both the state's attitudes widespread everywhere fighting between capitalist and communists ideology publicly criticised on their interest, badly their conflict brutally victimised many nations and territories even more than 2 billion people were dead due to their cold war, today they moved into a new era of ideological war. It would explain their behaviour illustrations like love story, here we go; Russia and America seeking to get more love from this Asian pretty nation of Indonesia, might be America gives capitalist souvenir but also Russia for Communist souvenir to buy Indonesian heart. Indonesia loves both the countries, can never give up, not enough for one otherwise love West Papua rich beautiful it will lose love, heartbroken, no souvenir and lost power. To build up Indonesian stable love relationship both the states must share West Papuan gold resource.

America is number one powerful state in the world; Lord of the nations on the earth and Lord of world authority of UN system, it never stop its global ambiguity to be forever leader in human universe. US reflected by Himself as a trouble maker not trouble shooter state on the case of West Papua. US negative attitudes began from cold war era until today after 14 years past in the 21ˢᵗ century epoch. It will describe a good historical distortion lessons point by point;

- President John F Kennedy Administration assisted by American diplomat Bunker mediated unlawful Rome Agreement.

- America controlled the UN to maintain world security, peace and maintain inalienable rights to self-determination of every nation or territory.

- America neglected to empower UN to control for security and rights to self-determination in West Papua.

- America showed its control fiscal and monetary system but led to corruption despite US funded money to facilitate the illegal act of free choice because the result was not in accordance to international standards in 1969 through Fund for development West Irian project. Why America did not set up any regulation to ensure Papuan involvement in the project.

- New York agreement does not concern which currency to use whether RP, US$, West Papua Currency or Golden who the Dutch prepared towards own currency because America control fiscal and money system at IMF and World Bank like American own Bank. Did US has discussed to Netherland as former colony of West Papua in where prepare to grant independence state.

Since a West Papuan leader Octovianus Mote and Human Rights Activist Jhon Rumbiak seek asylum to US, American has shown a good attention which the U.S. House of Representative has passed the 2601 resolution on June 2005. The State Department Authorization Bill also contained the validity of the Act of Free Choice. Unfortunately, this bill is dead, the government asked the effectiveness of special autonomy even foreign department endorsed open dialogue as former foreign minister, Hillary Clinton commended on the media. Today is the waiting time when Hillary Clinton becomes the American President since she declared her presidential nomination in 2015. Unlike Barack Obama or previous president he never spoke or commented on the case of West Papua.

Indonesia and America has grown dynamic ties in politics, economy and security but West Papua has been watching their interaction since Barack Obama became the President of USA 2008. Obama two periods had victory as president has helped the Indonesia's Victory for two period 8 years in term of ongoing occupying the Melanesian territory, this first black African American president proudly gives a big hope future political destiny for Papuan, and it was debatable case in the media. Many in Papuan prayed for 24 hours and fasted to Jesus Christ but Jesus Christ did not give answer, if prayed directly to God might be good answers because Americans only believe in God not Jesus Christ, if you look at it as US logo will find the word *in the name of GOD we trust*. Obama is not Christian and Muslim or other religion, but He only trust God by his personal ways as commonly many people do believe.

Russian Government's attitude on West Papua is similar like what US has done. Russia never has shown any human rights or democracy concerning to West Papua. Indonesia knocked the neck and mouth for Russia on their bilateral relationship even multilateral affairs when it comes to the matter of West Papua. Russia strongly supports Indonesia's sovereignty over West Papua, supporting military equipment facilities against NLM.

III. 3. UK & Vatican State (Roma)

UK and Netherland Kingdom, Vatican Rome have secret discussions before the territory of West Papua transferred from UN administration into Indonesia. Colonialism & Capitalism vs. Peace & Justice belongs to triple Lord of European seated on the highest position after God in the earth in the era of Cold War were Pope, Netherland Queen and Queen UK.

After seven years AFC, in 1976 UK and Indonesia bilateral investment cooperation signed for protection and security. Their relationship is long lasting, UK promised to respect Indonesia sovereignty on West Papua, in their bilateral and multilateral cooperation not to support West Papua independence movement. Independence struggle in UK parliament has little sympathy like in 2004 two former PM members wrote a petition to UNSG Kofi Annan, review the AFC. UK government through foreign minister interested to support peace dialogue not from Prime Minister Office, Beny Wenda, founder of ILWP and IPWP raised the course directly to Prime Minister David Cameron in 2013 has not yet seen their support. However, ILWP and IPWP continues to lobby and advocate, international lawyer and parliament members have been increasing now, led by two senior MP Andrew Smith and Lord Harries. IPWP as cross party political groups of parliaments around the world who are called to maintain inalienable rights of self-determination for West Papuan, their political declaration said:

> "We undersigned recognise inalienable right of indigenous people of West Papua to self-determination which was violated in the 1969 'Act of Free Choice', and call upon our governments through the United Nations put in place arrangements for the free exercise of the right, so that indigenous people of west Papua can decide democratically their own future, in accordance with international standards of human rights, the principle of international law, and the Charter of the United Nations."

ILWP is a cross legal party groups who consists of international lawyer around the world, that body functioning provides legal inquiry advice on the case of West Papua at the ICJ and ICC. Both the party is based in UK, now coming with a West Papua umbrella groups which is United Liberation Movement for West Papua has more stronger for legal process of the political and legal status of West Papua.

Vatican State is the only observer status at United Nations General Assembly and Advisory body of UN System then Pope is the important person at the UN system. Vatican Government has strong record to maintain peace and justice to save people in the colonial and armed conflict countries and territories like Timor Leste. Vatican state actively monitors the world situation such as war or any particular global matter, however, some critics say that Vatican also shows discriminative in their action; Vatican is more active if population in the armed conflict countries or territories majority are Catholic. Despite the fact that half of Native West Papuan population is Catholic followers 47% has not given Vatican official support so West Papuan people have been discriminated by the Vatican Government. Senegal government backed OPM leader, Late Beni Tanghama and Dr Otto Ondawame did direct advocacy to officials. Until present era, Vatican negative behaviour still has been though this marginalised group have been asking longer time never heard this God created people's tears and crying, obviously Vatican has a strong relationship to the military government of Indonesia.

Many people argue that that the use of local and national Catholic authority to convince the Vatican state would be better. The Five Bishop and Jakarta Cardinal definitely are deaf to hearing their people suffer and victims to stand up and speak up to world catholic leader as their good reaction and pay moral obligation. West Papuan prominent Catholic leader, Dr Neles Tebay had directly asked two former Pope on the peace and humanitarian concern in West Papua during his study at number first Catholic University, there was no positive response, and finally Tebay formed Papua Peace Network to promote a peace dialogue in terms of seeking greater catholic network. Some Catholic NGOs at UN promoting peace dialogue unless Vatican government reaction, even Catholic private properties broke for example Pugodide Catholic Church broken down in 2012 and many Catholic priests have ever been persecuted like Marten Kuayo a Catholic priest beaten and Jailed him in Enarotali 2010. In 2015 severe Catholic nun, monk and priest were arrested by INP during peace protest when they ask Indonesian government takes responsibility on human rights abuses; Jayapura Bishop disappointed these Catholic officials' demonstrants and Vatican government also still silent. It is a true proof that Catholic authority support Indonesian militarism in West Papua.

III.4. JAPAN AND CHINA

China and Japan are two powerful Asian nations in the world. Japan even had been able to control all Asia Pacific continents since Japanese Manifesto by triple NIPPON "Japan claim as Protector, Leader and Shiner for Asian and Pacific people, however, China never accepted because of their internal war and in reality only China became veto rights at UNSC from Asian country. Japan occupied in Indonesia and West Papua within quiet longer time since First World War to Second World War, during that time his work force system well knowingly titled *Rodi* in which many civilian had been killed and persecuted including writer's Dad, who had become one of the victims and also very well-known Koreri Prophet, Mother Angghanita Manufandu died in the jail. On the other hand West Papuan also helped Japanese people during Second World War, several of them were saved, and West Papuan elders became protector for Japanese and Australian. This is true history in the past. Luckily, Indonesia gain independence during Hiroshima and Naga Saki bomb by America in 1945. From this past relation one could tell how Japan is important to deal with domestics affairs in Indonesia. Why Japan is concerned about West Papua case does not matter, it is very essential Japan must pay moral obligation to West Papua. West Papuan people have to clear the past history that West Papua became protector for powerful nations during the war time.

Both the Asian number first and second states politically and economically are emerging to look for closer ties with their neighbour. Japan is the first biggest foreign traders partner in Indonesia with worth of US$ 30 billion in 2007 while China second biggest trading partner. After the 21st century Japan is more sensitive to Indonesian internal affairs including humanitarian, political crisis and human rights abuses for West Papua, Aceh and Maluku. Japan strongly reminds Indonesia to maintain human rights law into West Papua for example in 2012 UN Human rights meeting. Indonesia is very nervous towards the only Asian developed and powerful nation of Japan to show little support to West Papuan cause. China's reaction toward West Papua cause is deaf, China government more looks for investment and illegal or legal logging to bring out the resources only. West Papuan people also looking after Chinese people from the war, Indonesian government had given negative stereotypes many Chinese everywhere even West Papua, faced ethnical discrimination. Papuan China or mixture blood also support the West Papua cause including Asian Human Rights based in Hong Kong. Future relationship is important between West Papua and Japan-China; if two countries support the inalienable rights and independence for West Papua it will build a fruitful relationship at all aspects in the future.

Melanesian countries have built a strong connection to China and Japan in the 21st century. The 21st century state nation interaction is more rewarding and welcomed in bilateral or multilateral ties amongst Japan-China and MSG countries and territories. The first is the MSG office built by China while Japan built Hospital in Vanuatu, for this prospective West Papuan also gets good benefit from that service. In the political atmosphere, Vanuatu is the only country who officially supports independence for West Papua, looking for greater and deeper connection through the MSG link if West Papua gets permanent member at MSG.

III.5. AUSTRALIA

Australia is the first grandson nation of European and biggest state in the pacific region. Australia always plays multiple role and interest in the pacific political life and influential state in the black Oceania countries and territories. Australia's domination in the Pacific Rim seems to be similar experience to the history of African scramble or apartheid system these huge critics by native pacific community and many Australia's scholars wrote research papers and books. In other hand Australia is bigger donators' nation for development, construction, recovery from the natural disaster for the Pacific Countries. For West Papua, the economic development aid is number second but political independence is the primary need from Australia, reasonable question if Australia did to PNG in 1975 although their different political history between West Papua and PNG, why Australia does not use its regional power to do same thing and the best things for West Papua as well.

Even today's young AUS diplomats have a big worry to engage on the sensitive matter of West Papua independence aspirations because of Indonesia is its good partner and hugely populated state. On the other hand, psychologically, of course one can be worry as Indonesia is one of higher ranking military personnel and terrorist state. After former Vanuatu Prime Minister (Moana) speech in 2013 at the UN podium, an AUS's diplomat said to him that you are really brave if your small nation against big state of Indonesia the fourth world biggest state for military and population. Vanuatu is the only small nation in terms of islands, resources and population but Vanuatu can do big things to enhance the world mandate such big nation do for the peace, security and human rights. Vanuatu will show Australia one day when the West Papua brings to the Decolonisation Committee to finalise the independence sovereignty toward independence state nation like Australia. In the international diplomatic norm cannot undermine the state sovereignty, whichever nation big or small does not mean to determine winner and loser in the world political life today.

The first developed neighbour country of West Papua is Australia. Geographically and politically West Papua is located at central side on the matter of territorial, sovereignty, border, maritime, water hill between Indonesia and Australia. Whatever cooperation is made between both states concerns West Papua, a new defence co-operation agreement is made as neighbourhood state Indonesian and Australia due to some related to West Papuan freedom flotilla trips in 2013, 43 Asylum Seekers 2006 and regular smuggling even their public statement on open war. It had caused new Indonesian president, Joko Widodo reinstates *the old order policy on maritime state* after back up by first president, Soekarno PDIP party of course his daughter Mega Wati will dictate him. Indonesia by this maritime policy will control illegal arm trade to West Papua, monitor Australia, USA and EU countries' navy base in the Indian Ocean and Oceania or Pacific Ocean.

Picture 1: Separate Map of New Guinea, Australia and Antarctica.

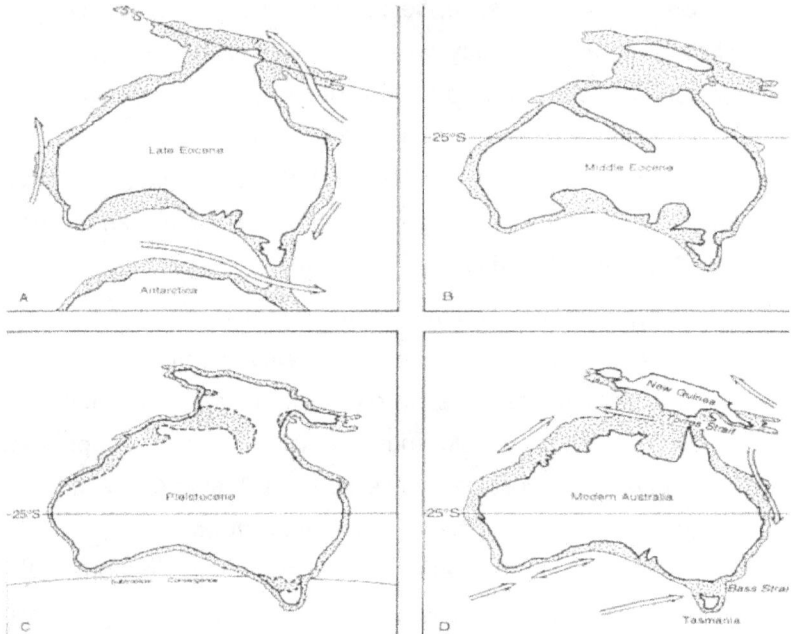

Resources: Australia Department of Environment, Water, Heritage, and the Art.

Australian educators Jason Macleon found three reasons why Australia sustain supports Indonesian sovereignty on West Papua, it includes both state has equal common interest against terrorism, corporation in mining sector heavily invested in Indonesia, supports Indonesian military rule for regional security or border security. It could be normal way if any armed conflict or open war occurred in West Papua will impact Australia so now the key question is what Australia proposes to gain greater power in the regional and international or any other interest. Asian Human Right Commission reported out Australia military intervention was involved as many people from Wamena died in 1970, now moved to 21st century era has also shown Australia empowers security force shot-dead Papuan. The currently alleged wilful ignorance after foreign minister was calling for an inquiry into the alleged involvement of the Indonesian military in the assassination of a young West Papuan leader, Mako Tabuni. Public outcry of the Australian underground people was heard that why their Australian government is continues to ignore, many citizens are very painful when they remember the history *of Fuzzy Wuzzy Angels*.

Australian government's attitude is more defensive, look after foreign ties with Biggest Asian nations at most; Australia's primary target is to improve their cordial friendship with Indonesia after China and India. On 20 October 2014, Prime Minister Tony Abbot without official invitation attended inauguration ceremony of newly elected Indonesian President Joko Widodo for closer talk about G20 meeting and others potential issues offering both states. *One of key point was Maritime policy that mentioned by his first presidential speech at the hundred thousand of attendances from activists, supporter, head of states, Ministers and other official quest.* It was much related to what Australia proposed to discuss due to a core impediment of the both countries ties, border security, Asylum seekers, unless West Papua. It was not a good sign to discuss for the matter on West Papua's conflict, only in their mind might see that Indonesia is worried and Australian as well is worried about their future relationship.

Australian relationship to West Papuan had begun during the First World War and their ties experience will never ever be forgotten for whatever reason. Physiological exposure such as human emotional feeling remain higher; happy, angry, jealous even sad and cry, that's all about humanity. Why physiological pressure becomes fundamental qualities for Australian connection to West Papua could be because of their geographical proximity, history, natural resources, politics and most importantly future outlook. In all those principalities are meaningful factors then West Papuan seeking and waiting Australia's moral responsibility because for West Papua asking for their moral debt, Australia never pays back. Although Australia's attitude towards independence struggle of West Papua gives zero attention, some people confuse even Indonesian very nerves such their foreign politics analyst highlight that Australia furtively supports West Papuan call for independence. It could be good lesson from their point of view: Australia backed Timor Leste independence, 75% Australian population voted to West Papua independence in 2008 according to a survey research, Australia critically controlled human rights violation in West Papua, Some Federal Parliament Members and 4 small political party plus Green Party are very strong supporters and their moral obligation. At the moment Australia just swallowing his sputum no response or reaction on West Papuan independence aspiration, we will see what happens in the few years coming whether and when his sputum will form out against Indonesia.

It is awesome to tell your future generation leaders about the human salvation history during the bloody war time. Do you know *Fuzzy Wuzzy Angels*, it is not poem, it is not dream, it is not joke and it is not fiction story. That history about dead and life for people and nation, all about future on your country, your saver and protector during your critical time, your friendship, good cooperation and your closer neighbourhood. Politician, diplomat, student, human rights activists, good Australian citizen and government leaders in this country, this book acknowledges you most of about fundamental and crucial aspiration of your next door people of West Papuan that about 54 years asking your moral obligation to pay back, moral obligation because West Papuan people saved your army, your nationalist, your parent and grant parent and your country from the second world II. What Australian government need to do is to help out West Papuan from the colonialist government of Indonesia and support their independence struggle to be independent state of West Papua. Think about the future in our region in the pacific, think about the future economic wealth and prosperity between both country, this RNRTWP belong to your hand in the future if Australia willing to help.

III. 6. NEW ZEALAND

New Zealand's attitude on West Papua is caused in various ways. NZ has always been asked Indonesia for a peaceful solution in many times, it willing to be mediator country for ongoing conflict between West Papuan and Indonesian government. New Zealand Green Party and CSO/NGOs actively monitors and pushes their government to stop military and police aid to Indonesia and asks government of New Zealand to support West Papuan human rights development and peaceful solution. New Zealand is also one of state member's countries who support the AFC result in 1969, sustaining West Papua integrating to Indonesia very long time. NZ and Indonesia relationship is stronger in economy and investment both bilaterally and multilaterally, their cooperation is facilitated by multilateral organisation of ASEAN, PIF and APEC for investment, economic growth and security. Economically, New Zealand needs to expand to rich resources state like Indonesia for global economy competitiveness, when dealing with Indonesia it is difficult to do any direct intervention in term of mediation a Jakarta-Papua dialogue. If New Zealand has willingness to help their pacific native community, West Papuan asks two political aspirations firstly to use non-permanent membership of the UNSC for peace settlement in West Papua, secondly as permanent member of UNDC help put West Papua back into decolonisation committee.

All the pacific native people populated in this respected country, a female West Papuan will prefer living there rather than in Australia. Pacific solidarity groups are growing well along with many white New Zealander and Maori, the native people. International Media in Wellington and Auckland did play crucial role in promoting West Papua matters every time, that significantly help to educate people on the ground and most paramount for Government leaders in the policy making stage. Then, government behaviour sometime is irresponsive, bilaterally having a regular discussion and talk when the time comes accordingly.

IV. INTERNATIONAL NON STATE ACTORS

The contradiction perception for the role of private sector and its impact interestingly looks at it as how much their contribution. It possibly originated from the idea that just brings twine good things namely prosperity and freedom. The local understanding about the foreign investment just brings good prosperity, wealth and job. Their ways of thought will be one of interesting feature to study more than how their local notion about the foreign company like a local well known leader said foreign investment will open up the core case of West Papuan.

IV.1. MULTINATIONAL CORPORATION ROLE

Liberalization economy and neo-capitalist hegemony through Dutch Indian Company extended after First World War, Freeport McMoRan presented during the Cold War, LNG BP and MIFEE are establishing in the 21st century. Cordial relationship between Indonesia and MNCs are developing well at least oriented to exploitation activities in the RNRMTWP. It brought core matter from the legal to justice and from the environment to welfare for society. Whatever agreement both the party made has always been regret, zero landowner participation in the policy makes level clearly broken international law, their awful legal agreement totally denied on traditional rights, compensation, and degradation cost plus not willingness to pay at all.

Multinational corporations are second colonial actors after the colonial states. Undeniably MNCs intervening at all aspect politics, marginalisation, armed war, genocide and destruction, then Haluk Markus criticised MNCs Freeport McMoran is the state actor in Indonesia. Their negative attitudes are toward opposition to WPNLM, creating disunity amongst all tribes and create armed war in the land. MNCs supply war equipment to support TNI and INP in the concessions areas for security. Freeport McMoRan Copper and Gold, Inc. directly paid two years US$10.3 million for TNI and INP security contribution. Because of decreasing payment, TNI is also involved in killings of two American and one Indonesian, seven American teachers and one girl wounded according to senior U.S. administration official termed to terrorist attack. This TNI action is obviously to ask money so that they can create war or killing for targeted persons such as landowner, TPN/OPM members, employers, foreigners or can create war between TNI and INP.

Second Deeper Mine Hole in the World in Timika

Indonesian migrants dominant in employments at MNCs sector, environmental destruction and ecological depletion. Learn from case study: Freeport McMoran is American owned Company, joint venture with Australia Rio Tinto receipt 40% from total profit each year. Many scholars stated *"West Papua has the world's richest gold mine and second largest open cut copper mine at Grasberg. This is one of the largest excavations on earth. The mine contains the world's largest proven gold deposit (valued at US$40 billion). The company operating the mine-Freeport McMoRan- is Indonesia's* largest tax payer. But little of that wealth returns to West Papua. Of the 18,000 employees only 5,500 are West Papuans. 80,000 of the 110,000 now living around the mine are not from West Papua". Indonesian National Environmentalist and researcher, Muhamat in 2006 believes that it will allow a huge environmental degradation, over 3 billion tons of tailings and up to 3-4 billions of waste rock will be generated throughout the life of PTFI's operation until the year 2040.

This massive American giant has produced massive gold, massive uranium, massive money made American got massive power in today's world, in contrary American Giant created massive murder, massive conflict, massive destruction, massive climate change, massive natural disaster and massive poverty and hunger to the native Melanesian Papuan plus open massive hole and hell so everything surrounding it is at risk of death.

Freeport is the king of master mind in chasing some tribal influential leader. Tom Beonal from Amungmee, landowner tribe of Freeport was Vice Chairman of PPC, one of West Papuan independence body formed in 2001. Mofet, owner of Freeport McMoran invited Tom in order to stop him from his independence movement; Mofet granted him a new senior position at Company, Vice President of Community Development Department. When Tom resigned from political leader many followers were mentally stressed. But a different history is well-known to the West Papuan women Activist from Amungmee tribe, noble Mum: Yosepa Aloman has strongly expressed her deepest plea that why you eat my heart, my feed and my lung. Tuarek Narkime, a key Chief of Amungmee tribe; He deeply expressed his plea directly to the Freeport Official that *"Gentlemen, I am angry with God. Why He has created such beautiful mountains, valleys and rivers, rich with minerals and placed us – the indigenous peoples – here in this place that attracts so many people from around the world to come, exploit our resources, and kill us?* Two revolutionary leaders were late Dr John

Ondoame and late General Kellik Kwalik have never chatted them by this bloody million dollar money. These two famous independence leaders never compromised with this full of human bloody American Giant until both of them died.

In the early 21st century over hundred MNCs offered to Indonesia for investment in West Papua. Statistically it is hard to count how many, because of some legal and illegal on them. In the report 24 global scale of corporation is stronger in its penetration at Indonesian strategic sectors that are also operating in West Papua in many years. They are British Petroleum; British Gas International; Canadian Petroleum Indonesia; Conoco Indonesia; Energy Equity, Ltd; Exxon Mobil Oil Indonesia; Gulf Indonesia Resources; Husky Oil International; Kales Petroleum, Ltd; Kopek Indonesia; LasmoRuntu; Maersk Oil Indonesia; Premier Oil; Permintracer Petroleum; Phillips Oil Company; Shell Companies in Indonesia; Talisman Asia; Total Indonesia E&P; Unocal Indonesia; Virginia Indonesia Co(vico); YPF Maxus Southeast Sumatera; Hyundai Heavy Industries; China Petroleum Company; K-Line. Statistical data on MNCs numbers are very hard to find how many in total due to there are not only 24 more than hundreds, secret agreement they were reached out without knowing by landowner.

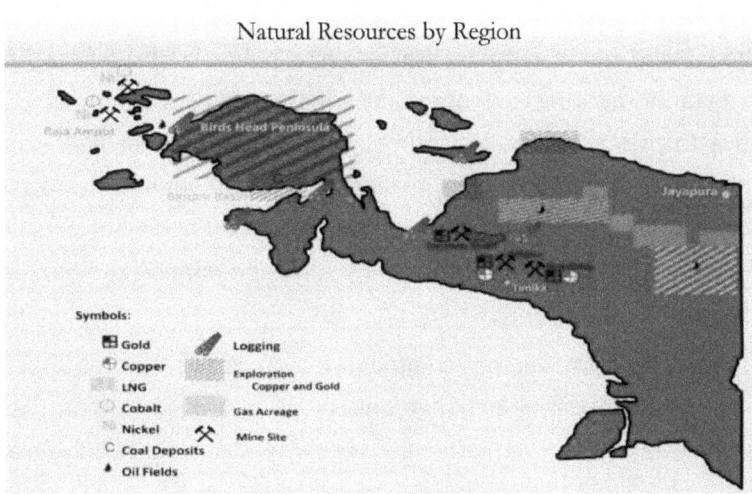

Natural Resources by Region

Symbols:
Gold
Copper
LNG
Cobalt
Nickel
Coal Deposits
Oil Fields
Logging
Exploration Copper and Gold
Gas Acreage
Mine Site

The illegal logging and legal logging corporation extends everywhere in rain forest country caused ecological crisis, inventor countries and Indonesia using military force to protect their investment security then massive environmental criminal act committed by state. Indonesia is the poorest mind, richest natural resources and third world's biggest corruption government caused by foreign debt blunder then consequently Indonesia has to sell natural wealthy Islands for their borrowers' country if unable to pay back the debt. Indonesian centralisation policy reminds control some strategic aspects; one of danger policy is private investment. No decentralisation policy recognition in the content of special autonomy law. The native community groups and provincial government are not part of the policy maker on private investment sector, the fact that Jakarta's centralisation policy interfering the special autonomy rule. Moreover, lack of consciousness and wisdom of these MNCs to maintain global justice and global compact values for respective landowner for their social security rights. Then by this discriminative law of special autonomy it allows whatever political actors can simply do their investment in the region.

In global understanding MNC brings jobs, promote professional, wage, training labour worker. Who made economic disparity between non-Papuan and native Papuan, who made forced labour, who made natural disaster, who made land infertile, who made family fighting each other and tribal war on our resource? Now move to privatisation all resources land the local government only do has regulator not as policy maker. Global market not only pressed local market in Indonesia but more seriously led to real destruction of lifestyle economically, culturally, environmentally and political marginalisation beyond.

MNCs are the key creator in human made natural disaster for earthquake, climate change and global warming. Human made natural disaster now very often and regularly occurring. Earthquake in

Bintuni Bay has broken down native people lifestyle and killing many native people after many years the BP LNG exploitation begun while never happen before. On 24 September 2015 hit 6.8 M Earthquake in Raja Ampat confirmed 62 injured and 20 house damage, it happened in next door regency of Bintuni. Another Earthquake on 31 March 2015 was 5.0 scales Richter nearly which cause tsunami to occur. Big Earthquake on 4 January 2009 was 7.6 magnitude impacted lake water level increasing victimised thousand local people and their properties. BP LNG activity is good example as creator of human made disaster, scientist research urgently need get there to conduct environmental risk assessment before late, save landowner and rich of fresh oxygen land should be protected for our human life.

BP LNG Tangguh Project in Bintuni Bay, West Papua

Despite international community being aware of this huge environmental destruction, but these investors has no willingness to pay their environmental damage and compensation cost. Thousands of species both flora and fauna were dead every year; hence these MNCs, Government and their other state holders absolutely despoiled the world obligation on environmental protection. This case should be to call International Criminal Court to examine who key violator was and how much their violence in accordance to the international criminal procedure.

IV.2. FOREIGN RELIGIONS

The definition for foreign religious groups is all the religions that came from outside of West Papua such as Catholics, other Christians, Muslims, Buddhists and Hinduism or not native ones. Native Melanesian religions are Bunani from Meepago region, Koreri from Bomberai and others in West Papua Land. Their interactions have not seen good sign with regards to peace development and tolerance values amongst for their service into people of West Papua. Foreign religion influence absolutely real and rooted into population's mind and heart then they only follow these religions teaching as the matter of West Papua will resolve in the right time. It is really disappointed, native religion is at odds or follow to devil, Animism and Dynamism though then they lost their true native believe system as their spiritual power that can be utilised to defeat their enemy from their homeland. Wrong teaching of outside religion incredibly impacted people's faith in their nationality, doing in many ways from the singing into worship; when people go to community gathering, In lord we are one nationality, we are one blood, we are one country, we are one human, we are not enemy, we are not colonialist, we are not destroyer, we are not killer even more than. It is absolutely misinterpretation on their religious faith due to their hegemony ambiguity.

Foreign religions agreed to maintain the land of peace plan that consists of Catholic, Protestant Groups, Buddhist and Hinduism. Despite everything they wanted to make peace on other hand, these dominant religious groups force have marginalised this native faith groups more than 250 each tribes who have their own belief system impacted their nationalism crisis, they forget to fight against colonisation rule. Their originality and identity is lost of their most powerful spirit. Some impediment factor toward development of Papuan native faith groups are:

1. Indonesian constitution only recognised five religions by political motivation.

2. No initiative of Papuan provincials and regency government to re-establish and recognised all native religion in West Papua.

3. Even special autonomy Papuan people not allow them to believe in their native religion itself. In this section absolutely failed the rule. It has shown marginalisation on the native legacy.

CHRISTIANITY

The most prominent non–state actor is the Churches with regards to human development, human security, and humanitarian matters, spiritual and moral development. Most people believe that the private sector's involvement positively gains a direct impact to the life of Papuan. As indicators to assess what the foreign religion have been done for native West Papuan mostly there are various aspects such as health, education, theology, social welfare, justice and peace. Humanitarian work sometimes is restricted with colonial rule, but they are very hardly achieved in their experience in who the Papuan led the Churches groups.

Only few Church leaders very strongly made confrontation statement. Remember what President PCC said in his public speech on 1 December 2014 in Vanuatu that some Churches did dirty political game in the name of God; they forget people are suffering and victims of the colonisation regime. Some local Churches such as GKII and GIDI against independence movement in West Papua. Those religions seem to be devil in their holly mission, nothing important to ensure God's news in this fragile territory. Conflict between Churches and inter religion groups are not new paradigm in relation to counter and support independence voice of West Papuan.

Catholic Church has double role in studying the foreign domination experience. In social economic development sector for instance, the hospital building and its services, school building and its services since cold war era until globalization epoch. Majority of West Papuan educated population was graduated from Catholic churches' of the primary to tertiary level. On the other side, foreign church investment is most lucrative in particular in the business sector. Majority of Papuan population been treated better services, developed better education quality including knowledge and skill in the comparison to states sector treatment.

Politically the Catholic Churches is the hidden coloniser from the political annexation to religion influence. Rome agreement was the secret history of how Pope agreed West New Guinea territory transfer from the UN to Indonesia in 1962 when Netherland Kingdom, Queen II Juliana and US president asked to Vatican government before the agreement was made. Vatican's attention on the humanitarian and human rights affair was disagreeable, after 21st century Catholics Pope responded that there only 47% are Catholic unlike Timor Leste 99% to help them out from colonisation. In Mepagoo region, conflict between Catholic and Bunani (native religion) for their survivor and hegemony unknowingly occurred in 1930-1970 as outcome many Bunani followers were dead in the fact.

Catholic Church, a Bishop of Jayapura Dr Leo Labaladjar expressed to maintain Indonesian colonial policy of special autonomy. Ten executive years of this rule, He encourages all the Catholic foundations not to intervene peace development despite his stated Catholic given responsibility to Priest Neles Tebay, a Coordinator of JDP. JDP organisation is not Catholic organisation; it is definitely peace initiators groups to promote Jakarta-Papua dialogue.

GKI is one of the Dutch Reformist Church actively against West

Papuan independence movement it is exactly pro Jakarta Church. This Church is the number one in the region, historically Otto and Geisler brought this Church on 5 February 1855 landed in Mansinam Islands, Manokwari, just now became capital city of West Papua province. GKI became second coloniser for West Papuan from in the two colonial eras the Dutch time until today's Indonesian ongoing colonisation. According to Markus Kaisepo, the morning star man argued that we have huge interfaith or religion war between GKI and native Biak religion of Koreri until Mama Anghanita, a Koreri Prophet jailed and buried in alive under Japan authority in 1939. In the book of Markus Wonggor it has been explained more deeply about religion war happen in West Papua between Christianity and Koreri from Biak Island, thousands of Koreri followers dead.

Religion is one of political actor, not true God institution on avoiding from politics at all their service. The Word Council of Churches is general Consultative status at UN; their political interaction is very unique. Today's era is that entry into new modernised religion in terms of more active involvement in *realpolitik*. From the political matter to Guy marriage, from environment to same sex marriage, from terrorist movement to NLM, all are changing swiftly because of global interests and modernisation influence. The world church groups play key role to convey the aspiration to reinscribe into decolonisation desk. In 2014 pacific regional forum for the UN 24 committee meeting in Fiji PCC promoted on this agenda but not Indonesian Churches do same like GKII Church in West Papua. Two reasons, fear from persecution from Indonesia military organ and working to contradict West Papuan freedom and justice aspiration.

In the early 21st century there are some West Papuan best well known religious leaders talented from the Christianity and Muslim background. They are Dr Benny Giyai, Dr Phillip Erari, Dr Neles Tebay, Sofyan Yopan, Taha Almahid and several others not named in here have also supported the independence aspiration. It is only a little good outcome from the foreign religion especially Christianity influence people who have good inspiration in national liberation aspiration, human rights defend and peace development.

MUSLIM, BUDDHIST AND HINDUISM

Muslim is second biggest outside religion in West Papua since the Eighteen century in Fak-Fak, South of West Papua. There has been an increase in the Muslim followers; the rate is now more than 2% of total native West Papuan population. Islamisation plan in West Papua is central policy of Jakarta, Central Government funding from the foreign aid in which that money comes from Christian countries. Muslim school, business, university, and mosque everywhere in this first Christian feed land of West Papua. Some West Papuan Muslim is Pro Independence like Taha Alhamit, PDP secretary and others. One of the Wamena man introducing Muslim teaching and insight in independence struggle, it is wrong idea to influence religious radicalisation into politics, it can bring sometime religion shock amongst believers, good suggestion is to forget about outside religion like many experience in African and Middle East countries, religion war and civil war because of ideology differences. It is most useful if they introduce a native Papuan religion which is part of the social, cultural and nationalism development.

Native West Papua's religion followers has been decreasing by some ways, recruitment Papuan child to Pesan Trend, Islamic School at Java. Current research stated that over 500 Papuan children were stolen by Muslim from their parent, similar experience had taken place with Aboriginal stolen generation story in the past that foreign religion of Christianity have done in the history. As Indonesia is one of the biggest Muslim country, Indonesia empowered the Jihadist links in two motivations, destroy native faith and genocide West Papuan. Islamisation of many children of West Papuan is core hidden course. In 2013 according to Australian researcher it was found to be over 1.000 West Papuan children from Wamena in the Muslim compound Jakarta for attaining Muslim school. One of the well-known activists has been introducing Muslim theological idea in independence struggle, then other Christian activists opposed him with their Christian theological opinion, however, their argument is completely wrong situation and it is very bad discussion might be impact their national unity.

Buddhist and Hinduism are not popular in political affairs directly but these religions are also aware of West Papuan suffering and victim indirectly. Two religions have also signed peace agreement with other religion in 2004. They want to maintain pluralism society to recreate peace to one another in the land of peace, all religious leaders interfaith endeavouring to achieve their program. No one wants West Papuan to be member for both the religion, they have not been able to involve in any violence; they are minority religion in West Papua.

IV.3. International Civil Society Groups

It has a great pressure by world society groups while the massive uncovered history of suffering and victims are still occurring, it really sad that the people tears upon injustice in West Papua is unresolvable and unseen it from the far or outside. The dead of many West Papuan independence fighters leaders after the 21st century, Kellik Kwalik was shot dead in 2009, Tadius Yogii in 2010, Theis Eluway was kidnapped in 2002, Mako Tabuni in 2012. Those murder cases underway without legal process and transparency for perpetuators, international advocacy (media, activists and government) to discover Indonesian colonialism practices was absolutely absent, and nonetheless there was only a little standard to protest those killing against human crimes. The NGOs calls SBY the

President of Indonesia to be public international black list, puts him into ICC to judge his criminal exercise to threat West Papuan for his 10 years his leadership. In 2012, an Australian based in UK raised the morning's star flag when SBY visited Queen Elisabeth, general public humour feared that SBY arrested during his exile journey because five prominent Papuan leaders had killed under his regime. If ICSG came to put more pressure on their government and legal institutions, they were willing to get involved that can be worked, in the certain time will be come through when West Papuan decides to bring SBY in the world criminal court.

Multi-dimensional crisis in 1998 after fall of 32 years of dictatorship president of Indonesia, Suharto under the great international tension openly have seen the conflict areas of East Timor, Aceh, Maluku and West Papua more openness and it has created a good momentum met their desires such East Timor got independence after one year later. Just West Papuan has decelerated their political independence aspiration directly to the third president of Indonesia; Prof Dr Habibie in 1999 after new democracy era began. His response to 100 Papuan representative Group of PDP said please go back to consider properly, it meant that given Papuan little hope for future destiny. Most people believe it is impossible to grant independence for two colonial territory within a colonialist state, if it happens, it will be a ridiculous miracle and big sad and angry for Indonesian nationalists scale.

The scale of world attention has been gradually growing by various society groups' participation to speak up on the massive of violations, armed conflicts and human right abuses affected to the native population in the country. The grassroots, civil society organizations, human rights institutions and journalists are interested to recover out this vulnerable circumstance to convince the world government. Apparently, development of ICSG tension have had contributed a series of critical aspirations, reporting and encouragements as part of public education and awareness even they provide constructive approaches that actually most useful efforts to acknowledge international government intention for the immediate reaction call. Those groups made advance in different interaction and activities, because of the complexity of the case, some of them promoted human rights section, humanitarian, cultural, politics, environment based on their organisational rules and goals. Pacific solidarity groups of NGOs together with PCC pressed same statement to reinscribe the West Papua territory into UNDC during the C-24 pacific regional seminar Fiji in May 2014.

Different part of the world has a greater support, wider network and connection from the civil society groups and NGOs in the 21st epoch. There are more than 60; some are CSO / NGOs with consultative status at UN and the others with nationally and locally recognised organisations. West Papuan never forgets their hard work for freedom. Given below is 62 World NGOs interested with the conflict in West Papua.

Table 2. Classification of the ICSG According to Continental Basis

No	Name	Country	Continent
1	1. West Papua Association 2. Tapol the Indonesian Human Right Campaign 3. Forest People Programme 4. National Union of Student 5. The Foundation for Endangered Languages. 6. Down to Earth 7. World Development Movement 8. Colombia Solidarity Campaign 9. Oxford Papua right for Campaign 10. Cambridge Campaign for Peace	UK	Europe

2.	1. Australia West Papua Association	Australia	Oceania
	2. International Volunteer for Peace		
	3. Medical Association for Prevention of War		
	4. Pax Christi		
	5. Religious Society for Friends (Quakers)		
	6. International Forum for West Papua		
3.	1. West Papuan Women Association in the Netherlands	Netherland	Europe
	2. Children of Papua		
	3. Foundation Pro Papua, established by veterans former Dutch New Guinea		
	4. West Papua Courier		
	5. Movement Peace, Human Right, Communication and Development		
	6. PaVo-Papuan People's Foundation		
	7. The Netherlands Centre for Indigenous People		
4.	1. Indonesia Human Right Committee.	New Zealand	Oceania
	2. Peace Movement Aotearoa.		
	3. Women's International League for Peace and Freedom.		
	4. Section, Aotearoa.		
	5. Peace Foundation, Aotearoa.		
	6. Christian World Service.		
	7. Disarmament & Security Centre.		
	8. Global Peace and Justice Auckland.		
	9. Pax Christi Aotearoa.		
	10. The New Zealand Council of Economic and Cultural rights.		
	11. Women for Peace.		
	12. The Alliance Party.		
	13. Oceania Interrupted		

5.	1. West Papua Action-Ireland 2. Just Forrest-Ireland 3. Tibet Support Group-Ireland 4. Afri-Ireland 5. Committee of 100-Finlandia 6. East Timor Ireland Solidarity Campaign-Ireland 7. Cuba Support Group-Ireland 8. Latin America Solidarity Centre-Ireland 9. Trocaire, the Catholic Agency for World Development- Ireland 10. Forest Friend Ireland/ CairdenaCoille-Dublin 11. Alternatives to Violence-Belfast	Ireland	Europe
6.	1. East Timor Action Network (ET AN). 2. International Physicians for the Prevention of Nuclear War 3. Indonesia Human Rights Network-USA 4. Papuan American Student Association-Washington DC, New York, California, TaxasdanHawai. 5. West Papua Action Network (WESPAN)-Canada. 6. Canadian Ecumenical Justice Initiatives -Canada 7. Canadian Action for Indonesia & East Timor-Canada 8. Canadians Concerned About Ethnic Violence in Indonesia-Canada.	USA + Canada	America

7.	1. KWIA-Flanders (Belgium) 2. Coalition of the Flemish North South Movement-Brussels Belgium. 3. Nepal Indigenous Peoples Development and Information Service Centre (NIPDISC)-Nepal. 4. Anti-Racism Information Service-Switzerland 5. Swedish Association for Free Papua-Sweden	Belgium, Nepal, Swiss	Europe
8.	1. Pacific Concerns Resource Centre (PCRC)-Fiji Islands 2. Foundation for Human Right Initiative (FHRI)-Uganda 3. International Platform of Jurists for East Timor- Timur. 4. Free West Papua Vanuatu Association	Fiji, Uganda, Timor Leste, Australia, Vanuatu, Solomon Islands, Papua New Guinea,	Oceania.

This international solidarity group's voice also to support a core communally shared goals of political independence through third party mediated dialogue and referendum which is fundamental values for the rights of self-determination.

West Papuan people are glad of growing civil society participation within new global government system especially international public policy making process but it usually depends on how much their engagement capacity into international forum level. The research show that 40 % of global policies made by civil society movement participation were endorsed in many case studies includes of Palestine, Mexico and Timor Leste excluding the West Papua then it is questionable about the capacity of world society groups to pose global policy makers on this territory. It surely is their weaker in engagement capability in terms of accessibility into global government system, for instance, lack of West Papuan representative organization into UN NGOs council to advocacy, network and promote the aspiration. The international human rights based groups; Amnesty International, Franciscan International, others raise up about human rights matter, nevertheless, most of the 1300 NGO & SCOs with consultative status at UN did not know and there usually competitively extend their self-interest amongst them. While in the regional forum scale, it seems to have been involved largely by pacific civil society organisations also back up West Papuan independence voice during longer periods in terms of seeking regional governmental organization assistance.

Chapter III

GLOBALIZATION IMPACT

BRIEF INTRODUCTION

Our world life entry into second decade in the 21st century ironically, the globalization concept, histories and impacts are unfamiliar mostly to the people from the third world countries and territories. Two society groups are marginalised and advantaged who have also drawn notion differently according to their experiences, insights and interest then the globalization itself no conclusion to study. If people have good understanding, comprehensively it could affect their insight what looks like the globalisation in their political life specially people under foreign domination. West Papuan people is marginalised society classification under Indonesian colonisation rule, hence, it is a must to understand their situation holistically about the globalization impact what the positive and negative force on their future destiny. One of the core features to analysis is what the globalisation consequences upon West Papuan independence aspiration.

After the formation of Bretton wood organizations now called the trio main international financial bodies of World Bank and IMF including NAFTA, the globalization was more broadly introduced into new development model of peace, social justice and economy in war affected countries and territories in securing its people. Traditionally this global institution provides financial aid for political reconstruction in some places during post war era then foreign government intervention more immensely takes place conversably the war and conflict made globalization more speedily into the inner villages around the globe. Under cold war reconstruction plan that was funded by the World Bank committed morally to pay back to the many post conflict places, Indonesia was recipient country on the behalf of West Papua through Irian Jaya Development project funded by World Bank. Under UNGA Mandatory, global economic order allowed to West Papuan economic development funding by Asian Development Bank who was managing under the Indonesian rule in 1969.

New world economy order pays greater focus on the private sector contribution in making global work investment, transfer technology, trade and export and import are global economic development agenda. It stimulates all interested party to play their game whether good or bad looking at new economic scope, capital power like higher technology escalation is driving force for exploration and exploitation of natural resource in which their target is rich resources country and territories around the globe. Indonesian foreign policy is *free and active*, its open door foreign policy opens the door for everybody mostly global investors, who are likely to invest in the many potential resource region of the country. There are some factors that attract the foreign investors they include big population, rich resources, potential conflict territories or country and ethnicity are driving force for foreign competitor can come over. RNRTWP is their global target country. It already became everyone's business in all standards locally, nationally, regionally and internationally from the legal and illegal business has been running not secretly. Few native West Papuans got little profit from the Indonesian government for their multiple benefits; regional governments and international governments got more benefit from it.

I. GLOBALIZATION DISCOURSES

Globalising in West Papua had a real impact on imperialism, colonialism, capitalism and militarism phenomenon from the colonists who empowered by massive technological development. *We must be look raw material. It is impressive words for all European nations.* Two powerful imperialist states of United Kingdom of Netherland and Germany took over the territory that was divided in two patterns in where southern under Dutch and the northern side to Germany in the 18th century. In the international political economy spectrum, the Dutch Indian Company's expansion in agricultural business sector made a good example to study how the process of global economic competition has been extended from the industrial revolution to global economy era nowadays. A general public knowledge believed a real consequence of imperialist and colonialist competition led to First and Second World War, a massive giant of US capitalist hegemony established in the land in 1967. Followed by global competitors for exploitation of the mineral, gas, oil and raw materials in this rich resources territory, this is the process of how the globalising West Papua virgin land.

Globalisation became a debatable matter in the new world order, for realist though the war is a key instrument in globalization discourse, people from third world countries argued that the free market is a key instrument, globalist said it is natural ways how the world we are living to utilise for economy and social benefit. West Papuan nationalist believe that the colonizers cleverly define a new term of global system of trade, wealthy distribution, equitable society, transfer new technology into their former colonised countries but it is not truly good motivation because the global rules has reconstructed their old colonial, imperial strategies in practical field to undermine the independence sovereignty rights. The global economic market system intervenes in the world institutions and the rules vice versa the rule of law is not a bible to obey it due to being created by human and not by God. God of Melanesian West Papuan people are Bible of Justice, Peace, Love, Harmony and Equal. Equal wealth distribution are part of the Bible values, West Papuan provide natural resources for everyone unless discriminatory action in sharing or dividend materials or their resources.

In the international theory the global phenomenon is generated from extension of philosophical, ideological and theological hegemony, for more practical side it was enhanced by international global theory of global political actor groups, one of them is religious or faith group. The Western religion of Christianity and other religion of Islam, Hinduism and Buddhist influences are understandable and reality of what and how they have shaped the globalisation is working through on. West Papua New Guinea Island divided in two patterns in where Southern took over Dutch expanded the Catholic and Northern took over Germany expanded protestant. *The Germany missionaries, Otto and Geisler established their Christianity hegemony in 1855 at Mansinam Island, Dutch's Catholic Priest Tilmans found* the Catholic at the Central highland of West Papua in Paniai 1926, Catholic expansion before Shoutern of West Papua in Merauke in the 18th century. Muslim established in 1882 Fakfak, Buddhist and Hinduism in Jayapura after Indonesian occupation. These religious interactions are diverse including teaching and social and economic activities to the West Papuan people more developing.

The global economy system in relation to market, trade, and investment took over by private sector. Whole governments work hard to set up more robust rules and policies, in the new world order much more addressed importance of global private market contribution but government unable to control their illusive activities, civil society groups more actively protest against the privatisation rule because private sector controls the law and politics itself. In this situation, private sectors gain a great opportunity in meddling with the political policy at domestic and global level. The government themselves cannot control global order, it must have non-state actors as the Government is sometime very weak to create the job and employment, not enough fund to do their own business despite politicians' public speech promised to create more jobs and employment to reduce unemployment and poverty, grow small business these all old ideas, unrealised. In national and local arena; West Papua province governor, Abraham Ataruri and former Papuan Province Barnabas Suebu were forced native West Papuan to accept global economic reality. Both the governor commented on media that investment is helpful way because people can get job, income, tax, social security like compensation. Their thought is old theoretical, they have lack of critical thinking and negotiation ability in struggle for equal global justice system, for instance offers their investment partner for 50-50 rate base. Barnabas and Abraham with their stupidity insight and zero intellectual ability do not know how much two provinces will get from it. Special autonomy law ensured 70% potential sector (oil, gas, mining and mineral) going to central government. Even in nationally, Central Government of Jakarta also weakness of bargaining power to the foreign investment sector, Indonesia only have bargain ability for their colonisation politics oppose powerless people of West Papua. Indonesia is not independent sovereign nation if dictated by foreign alien, killing minority people have strong muscle but killing this foreign party low muscle.

Government funding billion dollars in private sector development conversely government borrow from private sector for example private Bank when deficit fund to their own reserve bank. Community has not allowed borrowing money in big sums for social justice service. Government funding billion dollars through loans to the corporation or MNCs for investment needs because the private is more efficient and accountable. In this situation people cannot say this robust policy for all stakeholders and community, good for government and private themselves. In the local economy situation,

Indonesian and provincial government does not provide soft loans to develop native owned business development, there is no community development bank to stimulate local people in their business development unlikely in India, Bangladesh and other developing countries. Micro Finance System is a global economy plan to reduce poverty and increase the economic growth of some countries, as it has got good outcome in the 21st century, West Papua is very potential country economically; local people have their own business talent if Indonesian willing to empower them during past 54 years, there is no micro finance system program for economic wellbeing in West Papua. Take one example, private bank and Papua bank provide soft loans with higher interest rate in short term returning time is not fair while social injustices are rooted underground.

The rapid economic globalisation impact to the political conflict between Indonesian government and West Papuan people is overwhelmingly risky. The *Free Market* and *Trade Liberalisation* for both substantial subsequent factors forced into their struggle force fraction. West Papuan side definitely facing twine solid impediments firstly fighting for political economy globalization force or capitalism power, secondly struggle ends colonialism force or militarism power, oppositely Indonesia has always luckily manoeuvre this potential economic globalisation force for their domestic political integrity and stability interest more stronger rather than the national economic growth. West Papuan minority voice has always been stacked under the global competitiveness force, Indonesia sold out the issue of Papua to the global competitors, the key point from all their global arrangement is no intervention on the matter of Papuan separatist, agreed these big global competitions counter the separatism issue. This global economic force has had useful political tools maintaining colonialist hegemony; gain a stronger power from it to opposite the minority group who has a less power.

Globalisation is spreading the poverty, economy crisis and conflict in the third world nations gaining the experience from African to Latin American, from Asian to Black Oceania since private corporation allowing them to be a key player into new global economy order. This social phenomenon also has been massively stirring in the RNRTWP. Two landowner tribes of Freeport McMoran concession area namely Amungmee and Kamoro people income less than $ 1 US per day even reduce to minus level. It is very critical measurement to the poverty level affected by the private corporation that never ensured their social security benefit. Many of them die because of hungry and malnutrition. The conflict between Dani and Amungmee tribes and also amongst seven Koteka Tribes surrounding Freeport McMoran are result of the social inequality and injustice, this American huge giant used Indonesian people and other migrant to oppressed native tribal community in different situation.

The globalisation force both economically and politically has helped more to Indonesia than the West Papuan. The capitalists and colonialists intervention is more dominant to the domestic affairs does not matter whatever the outside interference is good or bad. Indonesia possesses a mutual interest in sustaining global ties with foreign nations by dealing foreign aid project, trade and investment. It has seen disparity and gap between Jakarta and two provinces in West Papua for global justice benefit going through on hardly to ensure what the locals wants and aspirations in better treatment for economy growth and social security. Even with new world order in which Indonesian government translating with their own policy of special autonomy on recognising the indigenous rights, West Papuan was rejected by some core factors; unrepresentative agreements, Jakarta and West Papua their historical distinction, corruption national authority, lack of interested stakeholder participation in policy making level and Indonesian top down national policy. In other hand, a Papuan Governor, Lukas Enembe has confronted the Indonesian president SBY on May 2014 for new special autonomy plus rule on economy aspect. All economy and investment program absolutely opposite with his proposal recommendations such as 70% natural resource revenue must return for provincial government only 30 % is going to Central Government. Jakarta does not accept provincial government proposal, if West Papuan gets 70% will affect Indonesian national economy, Indonesia always takes a serious anticipation that if West Papuan will have much money there is easy funding for their independence movement because they can allocate from the provincial budget and personal contribution to support WPNLM.

Corporate economic globalisation has been rapidly entering into national and local arena. Economy growth again 17 point resolution on Governor Enembe added Smelter project who initiated by Freeport McMoran must establish in Papua province to stimulate economic development but Jakarta wants to establish Java with unreliable reason, finally he promised if not accepted his idea Enembe will resign from his gubernatorial position. West Papuan independence politicians of nationalist point of view totally disagree with whatever economic or investment business running under the two Indonesian provinces in West Papua territory. West Papuan people have rights to manage their own resources by their own self-government for wealth and growth.

Global competitiveness form is a new neo-liberalization phenomenon that has been growing or pretty model of the 21st century in political economic atmosphere. Multiple global competitors include government, non-government and private actors who paved high wave in their interaction. It consists of two core ambitions that are establishing their global power of economics, security and political; secondly pose the local competitors groups and marginalised native community via new model of IPE. Indonesia has a stronger link to this global competitors for foreign investment benefit, oppositely not doing foreign aid projects to deliver the two Indonesian provinces in West Papua, in most of the cases the foreign government is always unable to engage West Papua's worst circumstance for ensuring monitoring and assessment on their social security and environmental protection obligation.

In context of global political interaction the global humanitarian agencies is a good agent to control their activities in most fragile states for reporting situation when government became weaker. UN development organizations does not allow developing the human security and human rights agenda but they have duty only to provide consultancy and technical assistance, limited to monitor and reporting its implication. Connection between UN global agencies and national or local authorities make fair for global justice development, in other words it is how to apply the global justice values to the all society level in Indonesia in particular the people in the conflict region of West Papua. It must to transparent not a secret on how the 10 global compact principles norms could work for better treatment of the native people in the territory. It cannot be prohibited by national authority or bureaucracy to adopt and its implementation for this global justice system. ILO has been trying to accommodate private partner for more than 300.000 labour health services of HIV AIDS, that is good example if ILO priorities Papuan workers although in very small number.

The effects and causes discourses to be visible when one understands how the global competitiveness could impact the traditional political life. If talking about global competitiveness, traditionally people sometimes understand technological and industrial development, states sector interests and private sector rather than local interest. Of course they learned from their experience, West Papuan people against global economic power competition before the core case is resolved by peaceful and dignify manner.

1.1. GLOBAL ECONOMIC COMPETITION

Indonesia is one of the richest countries consisting of 17,000 Islands or best known as archipelago nation; West Papua contributes main national natural wealthy from 5000 smallest island abounding the main land. To explore these resources there is less of capital capacity from the production to marketing then Indonesia must seek foreign partners their developed nations allies, it is not wrong for investment and trade propose and it is not wrong if global competitor groups (states, international government, TNCs, Transnational Organisation, Educational & Research Institution and Faith Institutions) coming along to compete into production market. These groups have their own multiple benefits from it, when those globalist groups deal with the conflict of West Papua but there is no negative risk for them when they indicate back the conflict resolution program will have negative risk. They are also running their economic activities even participating in national economy policy making process including domestic politics, backing political party in Jakarta and two provincial governments in West Papua. The special autonomy policy supported by all the above groups which defend more for Jakarta benefit; the investment, fiscal, monetary and foreign affairs not accommodated to the West Papuan development needs including their independence voice.

MNC of Freeport Indonesia and Government has taken a long dialogue for the economic growth and global social justice program. Smelter industry is part of social security in the global economic order that MNCs obligate to pay, it must establish wherein the operation takes place in order to get good benefit for landowner. Jakarta Government, Freeport Indonesia and Papua Provincial government debated on their different views; Governor of Papua Enembe, Smelter project must to establish in Timika to stimulate local economy development but Jakarta and Freeport want establish in Java (Gresik). Why Gresik, Japan MNC incorporation to Indonesia already constructed the smelter industry several years ago estimated will start operates in 2017. Final agreement reached agreed into two places Gresik and Papua province. Many people disappointed with this decision to Governor that why he has promised in public that if not accepted He will resign from his gubernatorial position. However, West Papuan politician or nationalist prospective disagree with whatever economic or investment business running into Indonesian provinces into West Papua territory. West Papuan strongly believes that Governor does not belong to West Papua because provincial government only maintaining and expanding Indonesian colonial administration.

Indonesia is emerging power economically after Indonesia joining in many multilateral governmental organisations (APEC, G20, and G77) in which they are ready to compete in the arena of political economy both regionally and internationally. Indonesia has plans to increase more foreign investment in 2014. According to the news, it consists of private investment and public over 60 foreign investors. Foreign investment in West Papua is crucially lucrative place. In the West Papua and Papua Foreign Investment Forum was held in Jakarta on Thursday February 2015 conducted by Indonesian National Investment Coordination Body (INICB) aimed to escalation for the investment realisation in easternmost provinces of Indonesia. Their core expected point into result is integrating One Door United Service (ODUS). INICB database has seen 22 regencies in Papua provinces while 11 regencies and city council in West Papua province has not yet established the ODUS but it should be done in the near future.

By Indonesian centralised economic development policy enforcing in the region, provincial government and native community became powerless, hence, through this policy whoever global competitor for investment activities is definitely lucky and accessible. Central government certification is determinism factor because of gaining local government certification only formality. MIFEE project consists of 30 companies in Merauke found some of them no regency government certification running the projects; landowner is central government not native people. It is only one example of weakness of the rule of law enforcement on investment sector led to marginalisation and tribal war. These companies have plenty promised with their unrealised programs to the native people, the landowner differently.

Table 3. MNCs Data by Resources and Status.

Company Name	Country	Resource	Where in W.Papua	Status
BP	UK	LNG	Bintuni Bay: Tangguh Unit	In Operation
Conoco Phillips	USA	LNG	Warim	Exploratory
CNOOC	China	LNG	Bintuni Bay: Tangguh Unit	In Operation
ECR minerals	UK	Gold	Darewo River	In Operation
Freeport McMoran	USA	Gold and Copper	Timika: Grasberg Mine	In Operation
Hiligrove Resources	Australia	Gold	Birds Head Peninsula	Exploratory
Killara Resources	Australia	Coal	Birds Head Peninsula	New Announcement
KG	Japan	LNG	Bintuni Bay: Tangguh Unit	In Operation
Painai Gold	Australia	Gold	Darewo River	In Operation
PT Akram Resources	Indonesia	Gold	Birds Head Peninsula	Exploratory
PT Anugerah Surya Indontama	Indonesia	Nickel & Cobalt	Raja Amput: Kawe Island	In Operation
PT Anugerah Surya Pratuma	Indonesia	Nickel & Cobalt	Raja Amput: Manuran Island	In Operation
PT Kawei Sejahtera	Indonesia	Nickel & Cobalt	Raja Amput: Kawe Island	In Operation
MI Berau	Japan	LNG	Bintuni Bay: Tangguh Unit	In Operation
Nippon Oil	Japan	LNG	Bintuni Bay: Tangguh Unit	In Operation
Queensland Nickel	Australia	Nickel & Cobalt	Raja Amput	Imports nickel
Rio Tinto	Australia	Gold & Copper	Timika: Grasberg Mine	In Operation
Santos	Australia	Oil	Kau, Cross Catalina	Exploratory
Talisman Energy	Canada	LNG	Bintuni Bay, North Semai	In Operation
West Wits Mining Ltd	South Africa	Gold, LNG	Darewo River,	In Operation

MTCs are top global competitor groups in the globalization era. The sources of resources and capitals bring source of suffering in this beautiful rich land of West Papua. Corporation believes that poverty solution is to stimulate growth and create more wealth for everyone, which will end the ongoing conflict between Indonesia and West Papua. Are they promised to bring growth, improve poverty, minimise the conflict for West Papua and Indonesia? The past experience would answer the question over 54 years brought to economy downturn, poor and hunger, increased conflict tension and inequality income. These corporations threaten the native or landowner people like foreigner and strangers on their own land, further more there were very badly victimised in inhuman ways. These corporation threatens the Indonesian force like landowner,

landowner like their animal similarity what well known West Papuan prisoner, Philip Karma's book titled *"Indonesian government threaten us like half animal"* who wrote this in the jail and was published in 2014. Animal in local term using in West Papua and Indonesia context like animal predator, Indonesian army and police are the real predators.

Indonesian new foreign investment policy for the ODUS will be an entry to new stage although in some provincial and regency government is already formed. In connection with UN Charter for economic, social and cultural rights whether will ensure for population needs or not. Using Indonesian force for certification opposes landowner permission can be occurring, one of the problems in Indonesia is most of companies without landowner permission you can operate as far you have Jakarta government certification because in Indonesian constitution clearly stated all natural resource in the country fully and legally under the state authorisation. So many economist, academics and activists believe in the alternative investment treaty has to put place under UN body authorisation, the Ellwood book explains the Tony Clarke's critical ideas that only UN itself is appropriate place not OECD and WTO for control international obligation on investment treaty. Tony Clarke is Director of the Polaris Institute in Ottawa, Canada and board member of the International Forum on Globalisation. He argued that the old idea of globalisation in the 20th, 19th and 18th century did not bring social justice but only more violence and war, hence Clarke provides main principles of an alternative investment treaty that needed to be included in conformity with 21 century era are *Citizens' rights, state responsibility and Corporate obligation. An alternative investment treaty based on these fundamental principles would include the following key elements: Fair treatment, Social obligation, Performance Standards, Investment incentives, Public enterprises, Expropriation measures, financial transaction and Dispute settlement.* That's brilliant expert insight; some of his idea has already adopted the global economic order at present day, for West Papua as it takes time to measure on these, UN envoy on social security is the only suggestion to discover the reality.

Will the ODUS able to facilitate the answer to Clarke's theoretical opinion for better global social justice for this West Papuan people? Historical failure is a good lesson for the future, learnt from the past 15 years in the 21st century have failed to applied and badly threaten West Papua under MNCs and Indonesia their political economic force. Their roles, citizen, state and corporate were misconduct, corporate sector more dominant to control state and citizen for example Freeport McMoran, biggest MNCs in West Papua became real case study. Citizen as landowner rights was denied many people victims from Amungme and Komoro. Indonesia government misled their state responsibility to make sure citizen rights for social security fund and their secret places protection. MNCs and Indonesia collaboratively involving in killing people and species, cultural heritage place destroying. Local provincial government and district despite running by West Papuan does not ensure all citizen rights, lack of bargaining and diplomacy capacity. Physiologically, those who are worry about the local government is pressed by military operation, they are afraid of military, Freeport McMoran is *military or not real MNCs according to Mama Yoshepa Alomang*, peace prise award recipient on human rights in relation to mining operation by MNCs.

The economic competition and economic business sector between Migrant and Native Papuan business owner is potentially a hidden matter. West Papuan just began after 21st century with small and medium type of businesses at all sectors. The competition can be as called as business war, migrant community dominated the business market for very long with the capital who was empowered by Jakarta and provincial government since the transmigration plan set up to the West Papua. *One of the medium owner business women said I have very worry to set up my business in my own country with very dangerous migrant competitor, because they now I have plenty enemy, I am not small class business owner. They said West Papuan we only support for governor, regency leader but in business sector it is own the business sector given to us, then if any Papuan with medium class will be danger in life.*

1.2. GLOBAL BLACK MARKET

West Papua has been globalizing vastly with a black market system. For native community, it is very scary if it occurs similarly in other conflict territories in American and African fragile states. The grave negative impact it has is never being discovered and opened up the story, the people pleas not are heard, and dead body are not evacuated caused by various types global black market like gambling (Togel), Illegal sex transaction, illegal alcohol, illegal bullet and weapon business. These could occur due to the factors that are higher flow of transmigration, gold digging, illegal logging and mining; numerous of dead number, human trafficking, environmental degradation, cut off trees, open new farmer land, those problems are part of real bed risky of globalisation present in West Papua. The geographical condition barriers and inaccessible public services, transportation limitation is core considerable subject to recover the circumstances, nevertheless why the black market is accessible into every virgin village. The black market owner always uses highly equipped machines and helicopter when they enter and open very remote new villages especially where the mineral resources are centralised. The government not doing rights project to help people mobility in the remotes villages, open good road or infrastructure for conflict places. Even some government official takes material benefit from it.

This potential and strategic conflict territory has plenty of illicit economy business activities that have been expanding all over the rich villages. The illegal business of gun and bullet takes control of the land resources and wanted for killing the owner land brutally and repressively if they are complained or against them. Local people and NGOs reported that 5000 of 43 tribes have died, today on this empty land the military, MNCs and national company exploring out the natural resources of Gold and Silver. Australia's mining company are operating in the Degouwo wherein the strategic area of illegal sexual business is located. According human rights activists they said that many foreign illegal and legal companies have been involved in supporting the HIV AIDS infected women and prostitutions fled from Java to those places. He said there are more than 100, unable to account them. Ironically, those Corporations brought them to landowner older for sexual benefit; this useful modus kills the locals in many numbers in reality today. In their report said that 2 grams gold for one time sex and 5-10 grams for 12 hours, 150 sex workers from Java were infected with HIV AIDS, about 250 local civilian around the place stated positive AIDS according to Paniai regency health department report. This sexual illicit business is a real killer for landowner people, the Bar and Prostitution house is looked after by the Indonesian military and police. Local government authority became powerless; there is military controlled district government.

Local community do not know the knowledge about HIV AIDS then this lack of understanding, it is part of a direct effect for local sex workers and innocent people around the zones. Indonesia military force empowered Gun for these prostitutions to their safety and killing the local and member of Independence groups as well. Case study in 2012- 2014 found more than 10 local shoot-dead at Degeuwo illegal mining area, before and after the years more were found dead body but nobody reported that, there is no fact finding mission and investigation. However, local NGOs and Customary Council of two tribes, Mee and Moni counted 217 human rights violation cases in-between 2012-2014. Many NGOs, Papuan provincial parliament member for political and foreign affairs, Ruben Magai and Laurensius Kadepa, Paniai regency leader, Hengki Kayame also called to closed down Degeuwo illegal activities and directly raised those recent violations to president Jokowi. Their collective action was hopeless, Jokowi president has no reaction because of military controlled illegal and illusive mine activities.

Black Alcohol market has been secretly operated by Indonesian police; the law and local authority is not a useful tool for security and safety of the native people. There are two groups for alcohol market owner: migrant and police while the buyers or consumers are mostly native Papuan. Many Indonesian alcohol industries give a special label for customers, such as on the bottle it is written as special for Papua or West Papuan many alcohol industries made from Java and other major islands in Indonesia. Most common local alcohol is Cap Tikus kills the brain and soul until death in short time, more people are becoming additive. Why customer specialisation in drug production for West Papua, it is a systematic genocide to believe on. Indonesia forces and migrant strong connection in doing this lucrative business, looking at the Papuan elder or Chief to sell the alcohol for changing prices with their land or gold, similar experience was when Europeans made to Aboriginal in the 20th, 19th, 18th century. Indonesian has already learned from Australia in two different ways namely, for politician learning from their study in overseas and security force training in Australia. Many overseas trained Indonesian security forces are actively involved not only in counter terrorism but also in running this black market in the conflict areas such as Paniai, Nabire, Timika and Puncak Jaya in mineral richest regions.

Terrorist movement is a result of the globalisation work. Since both the terrorist network and anti-terrorist unit is part of global agenda, the war opens up again. The globalisation smoothly comes closer between inner villages and inner cities especially in the mining concession areas. Freeport MicMoran in Timika looks after by

88 detachments of anti-terrorist movement, behind motivation in the colonialist and capitalist terrorising the independence movement, Kelik Kwalik was a victim from this terrorist war between capitalist state and anti-capitalist or terrorist group as many credible sources assumed He was killed by 88 anti-terrorist unit on 16 December 2009. Globalisation force is a destroyer or killer for WPNLM fighters, government does not accept the definition of terrorist movement who the party taking part in terrorist action, government also categorising as terrorist group if any government body terrorising people should be better called as the terrorist states. In the international relation or globalisation theory the NLM movement is not identical terrorist movement because they are not global public enemy like exact terrorist groups. Why capitalist and colonialist states prejudice West Papua national liberation movement like terrorist movement, then West Papuan rejected it, most people argued that capitalist and colonialist states are true terrorist states against NLM, it is sensible idea if we look at it as the social reality today.

1.3. LOGGING AND ILLEGAL LOGGING IMPACT

West Papua is the world's third largest tropical rainforest country after Amazon and Congo Basin; it is the major source of oxygen or the world's lungs. Substantially it produces 30% fresh O_2 in our earth's planet for the survival of the whole universe including human beings and other creatures. The longing potential is immense. Before the globalisation, the region people with illness recovered by just going out or claiming up the mountain directly they get fresh oxygen for their health; it was a powerful traditional medicine not in the ancient era but just two decades ago. Elders in the West Papuan village are very much worried, as they tell their young generation that our universe is broken and dead time is coming closer, please stay in God, we can feel now to much hot, acid raining, unusual weather happening. Our natural body is losing because of our root and trees are cut off everywhere. Our Native religion and traditional values tell us that God loves fresh forestry and oxygen we are human being is as His generation we also love our fresh forest. Whoever protects the forests, mountain, land, see and sky they will go to salvation in the eternal of God, it is our eternal Bible.

Illegal Logging in West Papua

Two types of logging both illegal and legal in wider study but also can be different if we analyse in political spectrum. As the West Papuan nationalist claimed both the types of logging are totally stolen in the illegal occupation territory. Indonesia and international community who support neo-colonialism and capitalism might be classified as legal and illegal. From international law perspective it is illegal to occupied country would be the best to call illegal logging exploitation in the territory, it is what West Papuan stand on.

Why the bloody global company stole the natural resources and overwhelmingly causing ecological crisis it is core environmental problems. This rich rainforest country and population is well developed in their relationship, natural ties more importantly to help people in all human quality aspect. Do you know what kind of resources they brought out? There two resource are forestry and fishing; Raw material and wood, illegal fishing. UNEP gives warning to China's Company then in 2010 already reduced due to environment concern in the research paper and news but it does not believe that all environmental matter will reduce alongside because the local people said there plenty logging company from China present after two year UN warning for China.

Middle income and low income countries make their country rich from their illegal logging business. The illegal and legal logging company from China, Malaysia, and South Korea are massively gaining valuable profit from it. The stakeholders have their own report and data differently like Government data in 2007 indicated over 14 million hectares in legal timber granted, after three year later in 2010 has increased up to 32 million hectares the Government granted to MNCs according to Indonesia' senior official forest minister report. Human rights defenders, environmentalist and people of West Papua assumed differently in which over 100 million hectares illegal and legal companies have been destroying virgin forest in the territory.

Illegal and legal logging companies in West Papua identically military operation. USA and PNG government stated that TNI has been involved in illegal logging and drugs smuggling scholarly report below Sttot 2011.

> "Indeed, several forestry concessions are part-owned by military foundations, among them PT Hanurata, which controls five concessions in Jayapura and Sorong and shares an office in Jayapura with troops from Kopassus, the army's Special Forces. As with Freeport, military personnel are frequently employed as security for both legal and illegal logging operations, and abuses are widespread to all regions in the land. Locals are often deceived and exploited into giving up their land, and the military and police have also been known to pressure village chiefs into felling trees. Having managed the land

for thousands of years, local people are also subject to intimidation and harassment from the security forces if they complain about the logging companies' disregard for environmental sustainability. Conflict and violence often results as many indigenous Papuans, whilst not opposed to resource extraction per se, resent the logging companies' operating methods."

One of big impacts of logging course is horizontal and vertical conflict amongst all the stakeholders. Conflict cycle is those logging corporations versus land owner overwhelmingly took place it in the last decade, this criminal cases underway unless local government responsibility. The horizontal type's conflict (MNCs vs. MNCs; Land Lord vs. Land Lord) while vertical conflict (MNCs vs. Land Lord) in real cases after 21st century. Many cases study for instance tribal war in Merauke after MEEF present. The war between clan versus clan from these corporations missed their promise to provide building house, employment and compensation or they just paid in one family or tribal leader even much more cases in other region.

1.4. GLOBAL TECHNOLOGICAL IMPACT

Modernisation and globalisation began when the sea transportation was developed by western nations. Lesson from the discovery is that the world continent is exploited for the natural resources. High transportation technology from the ship to Airplane, from the railway to Bus way the globalisation is workable. All the transportation development is needed to make a global development work faster than it could be good and bad in relation to West Papuan independence aspiration.

A. TRANSPORTATION AND INFRASTRUCTURES SYSTEM

The Trans Irian road from Nabire Regency to Paniai hunted by many civilians since the construction began until now it led to higher level of the population mobilization within 24 hours from the village to city or mountain to valley. More than 200 incidents in two decade, secret clashes between (TNI vs. TPN), (TPN vs. INP), (INP vs. Civilians) even (Migrant vs. Native), (Native and Native) in median size conflict. Trans Irian Road is most common than the Railways has been enforcing by Jakarta under Jokowi administration. It is great of Indonesian political motivation to dent West Papuan independence aspiration, military expansion in the region and foreign corporation and lucrative investment expected to be present in the surrounding region. Infrastructure stimulates social economic development in the region while good infrastructures facility stimulates the military operation flow more high, criminalities and violence will be mounting.

Trans Irian road building project in the region are limitless from Jayapura to border between PNG and Indonesia, from the Sorong to Nabire, from Jayapura to Wamena. It roughly estimates 500 incidents counted from the globalisation – could be called to border war facilitated by the good road infrastructure. There are over 20 military based camp, severe tribes living there stigmatised the Cannibal and Separatist to which Indonesia's key enemy. Indonesia's security force is real Cannibal, when they were shot-dead people they eat human meat. Many eye witnesses stated that when Indonesian military eat the West Papuan meat they slogan that it is a delicious meat for eating, we will continue to hunting these until the end then we will be worthy in our life. This statement very popular in the conflict areas around the countries, they even drink blood of human body, they are very cruel. It is their tactics to kill mental and physiology of West Papuan who are against their enemy, the Indonesian forces.

These situations explained above definitely true evidence not blame or tale, not lie in this book.

Physical condition of the road is not well; access to remotes villages around the country is very crucial matters to open global market and colonial and capitalist interest vastly growing embedded creation of new problem amongst various groups, local people, government and private sector. Million dollars for infrastructure plan was not helpful for road construction, manually ordinary Papuan kindly impaired the road ask driver for their hard work never paid, TNI and INP kill them dead in the Trans Irian road. In the 1999-2015 confirmed over 500 hundreds incident, shooting, fighting, illegal mining and human trafficking spread out. These horrible matters, the local Government in Papua always have incapability to prevent it.

Sorong to Manokwari Central Highland Highway construction project have been debated in the Indonesian national plan some said it has passed a construction by parliament members. This Trans Papua Road estimated to spend around US$ 7 million for 4,325 kilo meters long, but the core problem addressed is the customary land rights, not easy to ask permission. According to timetable it will start in 2016, it will cost millions of dollars because of geographic condition not only seven million dollars. This project was initiated by military win to expand their bases around the region that is why it will lead the military personnel. If we measure the feasibility study scale, military does not have any capacity to delivery this mega road project, null result you can get because not reliable. Unless, they can use war knowledge into construction it seems likely war field or military training project. It is a very critical and logically is acceptable that, they want to make war with West Papuan. That is the reason and it is a secret motivation behind them, from the first president to SBY even Indonesian highest military commander every time announced Indonesia is ready to fight against West Papuan and whichever state party who intervenes in their internal matter. Indonesian nationalist always have a negative emotional slogan when concerning the independence sensitivity of West Papua especially claiming their political sovereignty rights.

Air transportation and sea transportation is now well-equipped in Indonesia. It is caused by many factors that maintain the regional and national security, monitor and counter foreign intervention and transnational crime on West Papua. Australia airplane landed in Merauke several years ago was real scary for Indonesia. Border protection is high degree in terms of regional security and bilateral commitment amongst Indonesia-Australia, Indonesia-PNG, Indonesia-Timor Leste and Indonesia-Malaysia. Weapon smuggling and illegal arm trade is also big problem in West Papua. Only two options of transportation, in which are air and navy base. Therefore, Indonesian warship has been patrolling for 24 hours around the West Papua Islands now. Indonesian airplane has successfully broken down the Fourth MAKODAM for OPM/TPN in Eduda, Paniai region. Air and sea transportation control is the first priority, then air force and navy force personnel recruitment now underway. Under Jokowi's administration has planned will deploy ten thousand navy mobile police in Sorong, Western part of West Papua territory, in the border between West Papua and Indonesia.

Medical and technological transportation development is always empowered to Indonesian for backing above incidents such as using formalin gas, or hired air plane fly to Jakarta or their targeted places in Indonesia. If those is not developed enough cannot happen because if they bring by footway people of West Papuan chatted them, it is logically understandable.

B. INFORMATION TECHNOLOGY EXPOSURE

It is truly an IT world today. IT has shaped the world's business, trade, and security in which benefit more concentrated on economic business connectivity. No doubt today in digital world, the digital controls humans, humans unable to control digital sometimes. This idea is acceptable in reality. Technological controls the world, political and security activities led to consequences, most of third world countries and territories like Indonesia and West Papua with the potential armed war nation have to recept this condition whether positive or negative. IT contribution into political unrest is a considerable factor, for the national security benefit the mobile satellite or other IT tools are useable to counter political activities even foreign diplomatic relation. Former Indonesia 'president SBY and his wife mobile ever had been hijacked by Australian Prime Minister in 2014 reporting by one of US' department. Oppositely Indonesian intelligent body states that Indonesia only utilises to control some potential internal matter such as control West Papuan independence activities, Indonesia also counter world leader's mobile phone to monitor the country support for West Papua cause. Electronic communication equipment is the security tool because the leaders distrust among them to maintain peace and security, counter intelligent information and also both the country monitor their Lombok Treaty agreement encounter separatist movement activities.

Mental terror because of the mobile phone, it is a product of the electronic modernisation and globalisation development. Interaction and communication amongst West Papua and Indonesian has led inhuman ways of all conversation. Indonesian intelligent organs of police, mobile police, special force and army are intimidating to the pro-independence activists, human rights worker and religious leaders. There are West Papuan leaders and activist Dr Benny Giyai (Chairman of KINGMI Papua Church), Sofyan Yopan (President of Baptist Church), Jones Douw (Human Rights Activist), Markus Haluk (State Secretary of the NFRPB), Buchtar Tabuni (Chairman of PNWP), Victor Yeimo (Chairman of KNPB) and other thousands of West Papuan pro-independence. Indonesia mentally terrorises West Papuans by

Mobiles in two ways by directly calling and sending a text message. According to Haluk, Mobile phone is a communication weapon to intimidate and mentally terrorise the psychology of Papuans.

West Papuan local mobile users were badly affected in their family life from their unity, economy and security. A wife of former Mepago Customary Region leader (Ruben Pinibo Edoway), Mother Yustina Badii said *"I never use and buy Mobile phone because too many risky;They spent much money, got mental terror through text message by Indonesian organs, plenty of prostitution send text message and other little things as well. She asked some elderly women from the very remote village that where and what mobile university you have graduated so now you can use it do you know what negative effects from it"*. This traumatic expression is definitely really scary in such situation, Indonesian forces using to terrorising native Papuan mobile user in order to stop them from sending and circulating the information about the independence issues and reporting human rights violation.

World Wide Web connection contributes potential benefit for information and communication in the political atmosphere. Positively the most vital tools are digital media (internet and mobile phone) for communication, interaction and dissemination the information in general. Many West Papuan activists utilise the social mainstream media for campaign, network and discussion in worldwide. Social mainstream media includes the face book, twitter, website and online TV, and YouTube helping much to spread out their aspiration of independence. The long enduring political conflict is more broadly known nowadays not like the early 21st century wherein the local and national electronic media and newspaper was ban to report out the human rights violations, military operation, MNCs activities, Papuan independence voice and ECOSOC maters. Pacific Islands Forum Secretariat on sub regional committee admired to social mainstreams media users to provide the report and pictures on

West Papuan human rights atrocities and murder. So these specials sub regional committee recommended PIF leaders to further discuss on their annual meeting PNG in 2015. Despite Indonesia cover off foreign media and national media, ordinary West Papua's people can use their talent to report out all situations, people are more talented in the 21st century.

Indonesia and their counterpart especially in developed nations had established telecommunication system to counter the territory for common good for them except native community. By internet, satellite controls both from inside Indonesia and outside country, to counter their activities and foreign investment. America, Australia and UK were monitored for Freeport MicMoran Mine in Timika, when the landowner took direct action against this company which was broken down Pipe line, those nations monitored landowner action. The helicopter came over to them to confront the native people in the operation area.

Negative side effect could be that of an open secret information, faster intelligence work, moral and mental terrors, blocking their link and hacking. From most of the cases they found mobile terrorism for independence fighters, human rights activists, religious leaders, state leaders and ordinary people are Indonesian intelligent organs works to continuing killing mental and physiological pressure. All the negative effect for the activists is normal especially social mainstream media users facing this tension, never out of those. A new negative effect is assaulting the government leaders; this issue was raised by Vanuatu Prime Minister, Sato Kilman his Ni Vanuatu citizen assaulting him badly by face book during ULMWP's membership campaign at MSG 2015. As human being, morally and psychologically are unsafe with such effect. He did not support West Papuan membership. Finally, on behalf of West Papuan people and solidarity, Secretary General of ULMWP sent an apology letter to Prime Minister Sato. His people in Vanuatu very angry because he led the country in wrong ways due to the majority of population did support their Melanesian Papuan independence movement. Finally, He did not speak at UN meeting 2015, because of which the Vanuatu people were disappointed in him.

II. NATIONAL IDENTITY AND POLITICAL CRISIS IN THE GLOBAL ERA

II.1. NATIONAL IDENTITY

Building the West Papuan national identity and struggle for independence in the 21st century are the primary boost for future fate. Principally West Papuan belief system though has stated the landowner is the Lord of their nation who was created by God. By modern theories and Westphalia defined the nationalism represents fundamentals that they were unsure of flag, anthem, language, lifestyle, culture, the land, and ethnicity. It refers to political sovereignty of state nation, autonomy government in more global or modern way of nationalism concept; it is actually not different with the cultural system. Traditionally, West Papua is fully qualified to be a state nation since the colonisation begun, West Papua possesses some of the above fundamental components, in western theory they could be called the *barbarian nation or tribe*. Koreri Movement and Bunani are the only two well-known movements behind, both are well structured and their strong leadership styles that their material can be useful to contribute on national symbol it. Koreri Movement from Biak Island has produced many West Papuan nationalist in the modern time according to Dr Richard Chaufild 2005, first nationalist generation of West Papuan and the morning star flag is originated from Koreri teaching and ideology effects. Furthermore, some of the well-known West Papuan nationalist who has come from the Bunani's family for example the writer himself and others whose names are not mentioned in this book, writer is careful not to put their name in public, as the Indonesians do not allow native religion to grow in West Papua.

Despite globalisation, modernisation and colonialism being the most powerful destroyer, the state nations building insight is rooted in their belief system on the Bunani and Koreri and others native groups that they can provide all meaningful symbols in terms of national identity development. Globalisation force, the colonialism or neo-colonialism produced mixed mind and faith, the old Dutch prepared the national symbol is assimilated into mixed notion not pure Papuan or Melanesian identity representing, for example language use: Anthem in Bahasa (Hai Tanahku Papua), Currency in Dutch (Golden) and name of territory Papua Barat. Modernisation is a powerful tool for globalisation, diverting nationalism in assimilation way in terms of West Papuan nation state building process. The critical point why their original national identity is crisis; Netherland only developed their Christianity and Western popular culture all over the region during the two centuries, but disrespected the West Papuan's belief system and culture, if the Netherland empowered the native religion and culture would be able produce all national symbols in native language not in colonial language, which has been used since that time. Every native item is valuable and meaningful for nations building objects. It will be part of post-colonial development theory after independence; nevertheless it will not be easy like Mali in Africa, it took many years for their experience in national and cultural identity building.

Markus Wonggor is a statesman and religious architecture, his cleaver idea of nationalism concept is absolutely pure from the Koreri, some writers interpreted that Koreri Movement as generated by ethnical and religion nationalism teaching aimed to form the state nation. Chauvel argued Wonggor introduced mixed nationalism that religious and ethnical side, one good advice from Ondawame introduced nationalism from the territorial perspective. Nationalism from all the perspective are acceptable for West Papua in today's society, even mixed nationalism would contribute one main goal of independent state nation such as many countries do have, why no West Papuan can recreates new native religion nationalism despite it being hard afford it. For writer has a bright future on this to be one of nationalism and identity development program when West Papua territory is enlisted to the 24 committee member at UN and gets the regional identity status at regional governmental groups.

Indonesia has promised through the law of special autonomy, that it will ensure the cultural and native survival after world recognition on indigenous rights, Indonesia was never given West Papua to be member into World Indigenous Forum at UN despite West Papua consists of 312 local ethnicities. Papuan Customary Council became powerless to empower their local entity for native knowledge production and teaching about Papua nationalism. From the oldest to younger worrying to lost, majority people only to talk about their culture, that it will disappear shortly but their strong ambition to recreates the native one is no in native Papuan even nationalist. Younger already has forced by modernisation pressure throw away their self-esteem and self-belonging. Many of them compete to be Indonesian highest officials and assume 30% likely to marriage Indonesian women assumed over 30 freedom fighters both in home and exiled are married to whites as well. This is one of risk for their kids, muse blood can think differently depending on environmental factor. All the matter for indigenous development nothing is of vital importance under Indonesian policy even social security, economic prosperity and cultural development, no funding to universities and other institution on this indigenous affairs for research and literature development.

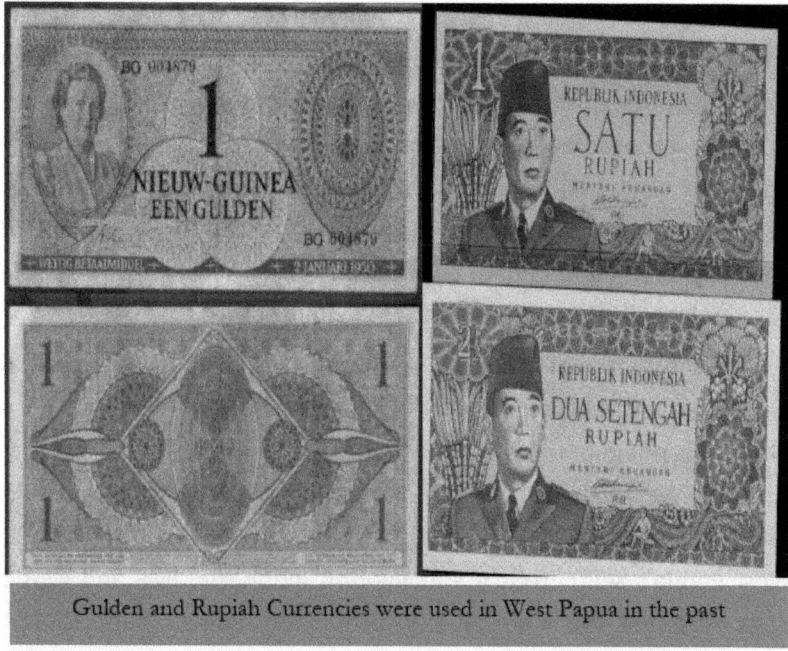

Gulden and Rupiah Currencies were used in West Papua in the past

ORIGINAL CURRENCY

Financial globalization impact destabilized the original or traditional currency which led to invalid in international economic financial transaction use. Now how to know the money or financial transaction whether their local existing currency was validated or not and useful or not, this is good time for the future. During First and Second World War era the currency used became core case in financial transaction in the region, workforce system by Dutch and Japan the local currency was pressed with two dominant foreign currencies of Jen and Gulden and just paid in poor salary for local workers because of slavery system. Traditionally, despite being a local currency, it was not recognized, but several places around, like in Paniai region used Megee in local market until the 21st century. The barber system was totally different in the economy transaction and the local current use in not globalization effect or colonization impact but their existing oldest socio-economic activity. Two colonialist epochs never lost their local currency identity even today is used in the removed villages by elders; it is awesome values that young generation must appreciate of it. Not imposed by globalisation and colonisation set up economic system in traditional transaction. Megee or other local money images were not represented in Indonesian rupiah and Gulden, West Papuan need to be self-independent not dependent and West Papuan people need to learn from the experience in many countries.

International financial authority and colonialist financial system both Netherlands and Indonesia did not ensure local currency usage, it is not guaranteed so today they using Rupiah in West Papua. Since the West Papua gained decolonisation status with the Non-self-governing territory in 1960s Dutch Government already prepared West Papua's self-currency equally with Indonesia. IMF and World Bank accepted the financial transaction for several years; UNTEA accepted the Nieuw Guinea currency of Gulden. Structural change of currency use in the colonial period also happened. From the Gulden Changed to Rupiah Indonesia. It was not an original name given.

Indonesia very likely used globalisation and modernisation in its own way forcefully destroying West Papuan nationalism. Today young generation's insight, self-belonging, self-trust about national identity is dispatched, more assimilated to modernisation and colonial though that's why 1% of total population is working in Indonesian system. Their ways of thinking is very dominantly Indonesian or Asian, this reality is principally caused by some fundamental unsure; firstly from the primary to tertiary school they are not allowed to learn about West Papuan nationalism (history and politics, anthropology); Secondly moral and physical force that native student or younger ban to bring or speak up for West Papuan national symbol such as flag, anthem and language and politics; Thirdly the younger likely to be modern style or personal behaviour; Fourthly their parent fear to educate them or give informal education, and fifthly, the colonial government rule not permitted to traditional culture production plan in the special autonomy law of 2001 including native religion, Lastly stolen generation has had similar experience to aboriginal stolen generation history.

West Papuan Stolen Childrens at Indonesian Islam School

Two decades have passed since the Indonesia gained a full recognition by former colony Dutch, people missing were taken in the main land areas. Writer was eye witness as to why his younger brother (4 yrs.) was missing at Kagaitadi Saturday Market on 15 August 1992 in Meuwo region, for everyone roughly assumed over 500 children were missing. From the West Papuan not only the children went missing but also the adults or activists case study Jhon Keiya (29) writer's childhood friend, He was missing in the Indonesian Ship 2005 said according to his sister Johana Keiya, many cases outside there. Why Indonesia stolen these children and the possibility of having various ambitions such as killing, teaching Indonesian though, Teaching

Islam, Teaching Jihat or terrorist like Foreign expert found case study in 2013, more than 5000 children Papua went Pesantren or Islamic School in Java and also in West Papua see the picture above. West Papuan Nationalism and identity cannot be preserving by doing such way. It was not advocated by Indonesian Missing People Commission, now how much the missing organisation motivated to advocate past incident under international global rule for missing people.

Table 4. Population Data by Elims's Estimation

Indigenous and non-indigenous population in West Papua[38]

	Indigenous (%)	Non-indigenous (%)
1971	887,000 (96%)	36,000 (4%)
1990	1,215,897 (75%)	414,210 (25%)
2000	1,505,405 (68%)	708,425 (32%)
2005	1,558,795 (59%)	1,087,694 (41%)
2010	1,760,557 (49%)	1,852,297 (51%)
2020	2,112,681 (29%)	5,174,782 (71%)

Elims's estimated population was very immense academic work that contributes an imperative insight for everyone; most importantly it pays attention by international community and people of West Papua. Native population has been decreasing and migrant or non-indigenous have been increasing vastly. Writer critically explains the demographic number for indigenous that it can be increase based on Elims projection but it can also decrease or drop down lesser than today's figure, it is sign of extinction. YALE university in US and News Wales University in Australia have had also drawn their research that West Papua population is the risk of genocide in the near future. U.N. genocide expert mentioned that the country like West Papua in Indonesia, indigenous population is at risk of extinction. Many research papers, books and newspapers wrote about the genocide, human rights and independence; however, one of the books written by Papuan was prohibited by Indonesian authority to publishing. The book titled sinking Melanesian race under Indonesian rule.

West Papuan National Identity Crisis versus Indonesian National Identity Crisis

Indonesia is a stolen state in the world. In their state nation building process has stolen significant and sacred items, which were gathered from all Islands, for example Indonesian Royal Bird from West Papua; this is used as coat of arm. Many West Papuan elders have claimed Soekarno gathered in his spiritual way during his prison under Dutch rule in Bofen Digul, near the Digul River in Merauke, Southern of West Papua. Soekarno journey was very magical trip around the region in West Papua to collect these useful items into their state nation building. In Indonesian national symbol of Bhinneka Tunggal Ika "unity in diversity". Indonesian nationalism built by stolen spiritual power from the different region, therefore, Indonesian nationalist said one day will become separate into many states, this is a very principal though provided to everyone, and a *senior lecture* of Indonesia University believes that the separation will begin in 2015. Writer strongly believes it can be happen then their unity in diversity versus disunity in diversity, each of Islands claims their independence. The first already attained independence for Timor Leste was last province of Indonesia, second last was Irian Jaya this second last province had changed name to original called West Papua; third last can be next after West Papua get out from Indonesia. What was happened on 1 February 2015, Negara Rakyat Nusantara (Islands People State) declared their independence, their political ideology and constitution completely against current Indonesian constitution system. These groups asks for President of Indonesia to abolish NKRI's constitutional law change into new legal constitution to respect every island or region in Indonesia by given absolute recognition for their own independent state. President of NRN sent open letter to Jokowi asked him to grant independence for West Papuan people.

National Liberation Movements in Indonesia has been growing in the 21st century not only WPNLM itself. West Papuan political aspiration gives a negative impact on the Indonesia national sovereignty and integrity destruction as a whole. Indonesian nationalism is not collective from the all islands in the history, West Papua was not part of Indonesian independence struggle history even many provinces in Indonesia. A book by President World Peace Committee in Indonesia contents Indonesian disintegration will occur after year of 2015. He provided the evidence of all NLM from all regions in Indonesia who demand their independence. They believe that their race is not part of Indonesia; they do not recognise they are part of Indonesian sovereignty.

According to Suntani Dyujoto, one of Indonesian political analyst wrote a book titled "Tahun 2015 Indonesia Pecah" (In 2015 Indonesia Broken). He strongly argued Indonesia will divide into 41 state nations from 2015, his some basic argumentation that ethnical divergences, cultural ties, natural resources, political ideology, religious ties, they have own flag, national anthem and its state constitution. Their movement is rooted and silent most of them, they are really committed to broken Indonesian law; those groups truly judge that Indonesia is illegal state and they disobey illegal Indonesian constitution. Secret link they are sharing and supporting each other, new generation more strong in thinking on their originality and their political believe from those liberation groups. Once West Papua have got independence, soon or later gives more confidence to other groups in their fighting back against Indonesia, possibly West Papua will help in their independence struggle. Those 41 NLM in Indonesia assumed to forming own state nations up to 2015: who they are interesting to find out and better to give them support to end Indonesian colonialism.

Table 5. National Liberation Movement List by Region in Indonesia

No	Name	Flags
1.	Naggroe Atjeh Darrusallam	
2.	West Papua	
3.	North Sumatra	Sejumlah Akademisi **Gagas** Sumetara Utara Merdeka
4.	Jamar (Jawa Madura) : Surakarta	
5.	Jawa Tengah :Kerajaan Mataram	
6.	Yogyakarta: Kraton	
7.	Kalimantan Timur : Samarinda	
8.	Ternate Tidore : Ternate	
9.	Sulawesi Selatan : Makassar	

10.	Nusa Tenggara :NIT	
11.	Republic Maluku Selatan RMS: Ambon	
12.	Negara Riau Merdeka	
13.	Kalimantan Barat : Pontianak Merdeka	
14.	Bali Merdeka	
15.	Bendera kesultanan Banten Merdeka	
16.	Bendera Kesultanan Asahan Merdeka	
17.	Bendera Kesultanan Pagaruyung Merdeka	
18.	Bendera Sumatera Timur	
19.	Bendera Sumatera Selatan Merdeka	
20.	Bendera Bandung Merdeka	

21.	Bendera Dayak Besar Merdeka	
22.	Bendera Bandung Merdeka	
23.	Bendera Banten Merdeka	
24.	Jawa Barat	
25.	Negara Islam Indonesia	
26.	Kesultanan Aceh	
27.	Kesultanan Riau Lingga	
28.	Sulawesi Merdeka	
29.	Republik Riau Merdeka	
30.	Gerakan Sulawesi Merdeka	
31.	Gerakan Pemberontakan Aceh 1953	

32.	Gerakan Sulawesi 1959	
33.	Pemberontakan Partai Komunis Indonesia (PKI)	
34.	Bendera Kemerdekaan Jawa Barat 1949	
35.	Gerakan Flores Merdeka	
36.	Gerakan Boneo Sabah Merdeka	
37.	Sumatra Selatan : Lampung Merdeka	
38.	Sunda Kecil : Jakarta Merdeka	
39.	Flobamora dan Sumba: Kupang Merdeka	
40.	Maluku Tenggara: Free Tual	
41.	North Sulawesi	

II.2. POLITICAL CRISIS AND NATIONAL UNITY

A. LEADERSHIP CRISIS

Why was the organisational and leadership structure of WPNLM was unstable in the 21st century. West Papua not to have a strong political leaders like Nelson Mandela, Sanana Gusmao, Muhamad Ghandi for West Papuan political revolution but it is still a wrong opinion. In independence struggle there were several powerful leaders that have been killed by colonial government of Indonesia and the others had retired like OPM leaders both inside and outside. However, it essentially reguired to find what is acceptable measures and qualities in the leadership stage inspite of their personal characteristic, behavior, faith, nationalism, patriotism they need to have it before led their struggle destiny for independence. The political leader of the independence revolution is different from the head of state or government, it is revolutionary leader who always be enemy in the public eyes especially to the colonial government and particular political actor could be private and international government, therefore, what the leadership style be suitable in this contemporary time, globalisation and modernisation.

Theoretically 2008 Wise has classified some leadership style that includes dictatorial, populist, pragmatic, consultative and charismatic. His opinion is widely acceptable now, on how to translate into independence struggle need more analytical argumentation before set up it appropriately what is qualified because this struggle destiny depend on what and how to navigate by the current leaders. What leadership characters is suitable to lead power in the independence struggle? How many leaders are recommended in structurally; diplomatic, military and clandestine? How to assign them into three leadership style? It is helpful to examine through SWOT formulation from above types and some basic variable can be useful are social and cultural context, contemporary global politics condition, and colonial system that will be cope the leadership needs. Military win might be dictatorial dislike and Charismatic in Calendestine based in home and populist might be diplomatic leader based in overseas.

One of the distrusted point is where the venue refers to democracy and election system. Most people believe in the European system, Indonesian system and modern style. Therefore, the ideas of what proper democracy style must be found out, how to design and implement it rightfully and it must be accepted by all interested party of internal and external groups amongts West Papuan. Whatever democracy system and its structure is to be useful if commonly agreed it will help to elected central political figur to be independence leader. The democracy system is touchable and acceptable if it is done based on the nature of struggle like all party involvement approach. Modern democracy system and colonial democracy is not always the best alternative, it indicated still colonial model of electoral system without vote by majority people or radical groups. The traditional model of democracy is also part of it. In spite of people accepting the western democracy system for their election every where but it is not always be suitable to introduce in some political situation. If using colonial ideology within colonial democracy and election rule to reconstruct the native Papuan political leadership structure probably be disturbed by some below factors in independence revolusion period.

   a. Disrespect cultural norms or natural law; do not use the colonial instruments in your struggle.
   b. Not represented by all population and radical groups due to distance.
   c. Easy interference by colonialist groups.
   d. Cannot have enough space in Indonesia because of strictly controlled by military system.
   e. Can undermine legacy and privacy for the revolusion law itself, intelligent easily to get information.
   f. Unexpected killings and jailing can occur if held in Indonesia.

Majority Papuan people seem to recognise only the open forum mechanism in the general election their leaders but it is wrong because of hard to accomodate all West Papuan both exile leaders and home leaders in this time. They have tried many venues both inside and exile in completing for their leadership needs. Take example from home they have found many times that it was a failure such as:

   1. Firstly, Second Papua Congress in 2000 without people's vote the leader was self appointed by himself, H Eluway by

his word he said in the forum *now I became president and my vice president I elect my colleagues Tom Beonal.*

2. Secondly, Third Papua Congress 2011, elected the Prime Minister and President by minority groups. By modern and colonial models of leadership election and its democracy totally inapplicable despite the second congress rumour used the native democracy system to elect their leader of Yoboisembut as President and Edison Waromi as Prime minister.

3. Thirdly, in Vanuatu, in 2008 higher leaders summit in Port Villa elected the Chairman (Brigader Yoweni) and vice Chaiman (Dr John Ondomane).

Many argued that unsuccesful upon all event because of some internalities were distrust amongts them, egoism, premodalism and hypocracy sometime.

B. Disunity versus Unity Crisis

Disunity seemed to be major utopia in convincing the public international trust and building a more stronger movement widely. The disunity is a dilemma opposing the unity is a victory philosopical insight, it simply can be explained that stronger unity will lead to stronger movement to achieve it. Disunity itself is a weapon in killing liberation movement power conversely unity is key weapon in killing colonial power. This philosophical notion should be constructed and accepted by all West Papuan as best approach to build more unity power. In reconstructing national unity of Papuan obviously taking very long process and not easy task in the colonial period, different characteristics amongst local ethnics groups, their strategies and motivation diffrencies in order to bring all groups into one united goal. The unity development principally required how much people's fundamental faith in independence struggle in order to assess their strength and weakness have it. It is judging about patriotism and nationalism, whether every single of Papuan citizens have it or not. If the patriotism and nationalism notion is insisted by all Papuan people probably the unity can reconstruct in certain time; short-median-or long term but the nationalism or patriotism diverted by colonialism force must be harder it can lead to two consequences, namely ways of thinking and self-believe as Papuan empty in their heart and mind.

ANTI-INDEPENDENCE GROUPS OR WEST PAPUAN PRO INDONESIA GROUPS

Indonesian foreign political strategy aimed to undermine international opinion and gaining wider support globally to counter West Papuan independence movement activities everywhere. Indonesian has pretty political strategy in using West Papuan people itself, they have two groups; firstly West Papuan former exile independence activists, secondly the West Papuan Indonesian officials then this strategy became useful as a bargaining tool that colonialist state practising it all the time. After the ten years of the colonial policy of the special autonomy has failed to reinforce, tactically Indonesia set up a new West Papuan Pro Integration group led by Nicholaus Meset and Frans Alberth Yoku, two former exile leader of Free West Papua Movement spent up 20 years. It's completely a very new political paradigm taking place, two groups elaborating themselves in the international and regional forum to convince government leaders that the special autonomy is the win-win political solution, then they want to gain foreign governement recognition and trust, they using in the name of social economic disadvantage and indegenous affair development.

Indonesian governement continuously have been empowering West Papuan Pro Indonesia via foreign fund to travel overseas every time and everywhere against the human rights campaign, independence movement, meeting the Papuan independence activists in their ways if they did not return into Indonesia to be target of killing. Two betrayer of Frans Albert Yoku and Nick Messet met Dr John Ondoame in August 2014, the both traders asked him to return back to support Indonesian colonialism in West Papua. On the other side to defend Indonesian colonialism in West Papua, Yoku and Messet agaitns Vanuatu Prime Minister 2014 they said *you only small country nothing influence in the international flora, all human rights record you have reported not according to true fact.* Both the spyman not only in one occation but also they partook severe regional and international forum meeting; case study in 2011 Pacific Islands Forum, 2010 refrendum conference in UK, and meeting at MSG begun 2010 in these forum they acknowledge the Indonesian colonial law of sepecial autonomy and asked exile West Papuan returned back to depend integral of Indonesia. Writer was one of the presenter at Peace Confrence who politician, activist and supporter attended during PIF forum 2011 said *please a little boatman better you go to study learn english first and come back to support us, added special autonomy is win-win solution on West Papuan conflict.* Refrendum Confrence in 2010 UK coordinated By Benny Wenda and Parliamentarian Groups, Messet also opposed in the Forum, but luckly, police were involved to control him.

Indonesian Intelligent Body cooperated to many civilian millitan groups. They are BMP, Angkatan 45, FPPKI and many others. Papuan Officials in the Indonesian two provinces and regencies government, districs and suburbs has been influencing Papuan civil society support for Indonesia's integration and sovereignity. They are cooperating with Indonesian National Army and Indonesian National Police. On the other hand Pro Indonesia Groups widespread around the world, their base is in donor countries such as Australia, New Zeland, UK, US and Netherland, Norway and many other countries. There are few number West Papuan and majority of migrant people who were born in West Papua promoting the special autonomy law and other colonial policies. These groups of people operate variety of activities funded by the special autonomy money who massivley come from donor countries around the world. Their activities normally include operating during the special occassion such as West Papuan national day and Indonesian integration day, those day is very worry because West Papuan pro independence frequently do peacefull protest.

INTERNAL PRO INDEPENDENCE POLITICAL FRACTION

The two main independence body in the two era 20th century and 21st century are OPM and TPN: The OPM is diplomatic win and TPN is military win. The first umbrella organisation is OPM (Free Papua Movement) before other new organisations were found. The OPM as single NLM body, Indonesian colonialism influence has destroyed this principal NLM body. Broken or divided the OPM has two groups, OPM led by Jakob Pray and OPM led by Zet Romkorem. Finally, they both agreed to work as one body called United Front for OPM who facilated by Vanuatu Government in 1994. NLM of OPM was divided into resistance groups in the 21st century are WPNA, DAP, PDP, KNPB and WPNCL. Each of NLM faction has its own history and capacity no one groups is highest or it does not means superiority, those who are struggling for West Papua's independence is the central goal.

Majority people critically asked what causes of the disunity due to multiple political factions internally or internal disparities in one side. What are the ambitions, take one example that there is various agendas amongst internal West Papuan political groups which is capable of distinguishing people though and trust in broader aspect. Their different aspiration comprises of third party mediation, decolonization development, referendum, and recognition of independence sovereignty. Formation of Federal Republic State of

West Papua 2011 became new phenomenon in the struggle, however, guerrilla war was decided as a final resolution if any of the peaceful ways mentioned above did not meet. They act variously and seem unseen good solidarity to support amongst them. Each of groups working on their own priority agenda are separate for example KNPB & WPNP for referendum, WPNCL is Decolonization and third party mediation, WPNA and DAP promotes recoignition for their Federal State and TPN/OPM consistantly committed to guerrilla war while the faith based groups and NGO/CSOs seeking for peaceful dialogue. They have a very unique position towards the main goal of political independence but are unorganized and uncoordinated movement both structurally and functionally that always been able to contribute an internal political ideology conflict.

This condition became a public outcry and it has visible when their motivation and ambition going to lead the independence struggle power despite wider humour indicated that several groups secretly working to support colonial government of Indonesia against separatist movement. There was raise in blaming between and because of them it negatively affected to the world community which needed international greater support. If the independence movement on that level, automatically anti-independence groups will growing bigger, international public distrust on West Papuan unity in independence. It also ever rose question by MSG leaders in their meeting. To pave away against this negative image, the unification agenda was taken as very potential tool to reacknowledge that West Papua is now under the united voice and unified body as an central umbrela organisation to manage and coordinate the independence movement structually and effectively.

MSG distrusted to have only one groups even the group was on behalf of many independence groups, all the resistance groups must accept this reality wherein the unifaction dilemma is no longer a weakness in the face of the regional government leaders. WPNCL was established in 2008 as an umbrella body with more 30 social and political groups who sponsored by the Vanuatu Government. Based on fact that WPNCL did apply a full memberhsip status into MSG was rejected it despite that was confronted Vanuatu's consisten endorsement but never end his new initiative for reunification because of MSG's Special Leader Communique adviced to West Papuan groups for a new fresh application and it must be united and inclusive.

FORMATION ON FINAL WPNLM

Three main political groups (PNWP, WPNCL and NFRPB) had established a new umbrella organisation entitled United Liberation Movement for West Papua (ULMWP) on 6 December 2014 in Port Villa, Vanuatu. Regardless of the President of NFRPB expressed his disappoitment on the media not to support this new umbrella groups, the great moment never come back again, will need to more advice him to able to understand the important of unity in the age of global. Another group of WPLO who this organisation already accrediated with the UN Indigenous Forum also did not recognise, despite WPLO obtained as special consultative status at NGO Branch at the UN, rationally, this group is not the political groups, it is still only NGOs.

SARALANA DECLARATION ON WEST PAPUA UNITY

We the undersigned; the Federal Republic for West Papua (NRFPB), West Papua National Coalition of Liberation (WPNCL), West Papua National Parliament (WPNP/New Guinea Raad), have conducted the Summit on West Papuan Unification at Saralana, Port Vila, Vanuatu, from 30th November – 6th December 2014.

In the name of the people, the nation and the land of West Papua, we do declare that today the 6th December 2014 at the Chief's Nakamal, at Saralana, Port Vila, Vanuatu, that the undersigned groups have united and established the United Liberation Movement for West Papua (ULMWP), a body representing all resistance organisations both inside and outside West Papua.

We declare and claim that all West Papuans, both inside and outside West Papua, are united under this new body and that we will continue our struggle for independence.

This meeting has been conducted pursuant to the decision made by the Melanesian Spearhead Group (MSG) in Port Moresby, Papua New Guinea in June 2014, that West Papuan Independence organisations must first unite before an application for membership can be re-submitted to the Melanesian Spearhead Group (MSG). We are now united and will re-submit an application under this new body, the ULMWP.

We are determined that the United Liberation Movement for West Papua (ULMWP) becomes the coordinating body to support all international efforts to regain our sovereignty. In order to support this, we have formed a secretariat of five people; Benny Wenda, Jacob Rumbiak, Leone Tanggahma, Octovianus Mote and Rex Rumakiek, and representing the three largest resistance organisations and also all non-affiliated resistance organisations that support our struggle. We will maintain our existing organisations but commit to be united by the coordinating efforts of the United Liberation Movement for West Papua.

This important and historic declaration has been made possible through the faithful efforts of the Vanuatu Government, Malvatumauri National Council of Chiefs, the Vanuatu Christian Council, the Pacific Conference of Churches and the commitment of the following liberation organisations:

This Declaration is signed at the Chiefs' Nakamal, Port Vila, on this day Sixth of December, Two Thousand and Fourteen, by:

Federal Republic of West Papua
Ev. Edison Kladius Waromi SH.

West Papua National Coalition for Liberation
Rex Rumakiek

West Papua National Parliament
Buchtar Tabuni

Witnessed by:

Chief Senimao Tirsupe Mol Torvakavat
President of Malvatumauri Council of Chiefs

Pastor Shem Tema, The General Secretary
Vanuatu Christian Council

Rev. Francois Pihaatae, The General Secretary
Pacific Conference of Churches

Former Prime Minister of The Republic of Vanuatu,
Barak Tame Sope Maautamate

Independence movement under the ULMWP now is realible
and qualified because it is the only umbrella body of NLM for West
Papuan. One step of the liberation movement already had moved
forward in driving their political goal, it has been showing greater
power on their unity before seeking regional governmental trust
and its recoignition. ULMWP is legitimated body of WPNLM who
recognised by MSG and is seeking membership status for PIF including
at the UNDC desk.

LEADERSHIP STRUCTURE WAS FULLFILED

The leadership crisis inwhere everyone were worried on the regional
politics when distrust and disunity concerned by MSG leaders, Vanuatu
goverment never forgive up to facilitate the meeting was held West
Papua Leader Summit in 2014. To set up the leadership structure it
has taken a long dialogue on the summit, commonly came out with
a fresh idea that formed a coordinating body in which structurally

has two main board are Executive and Council Committee. Executive led by five official consists of Secretary General: Octovinaus Mote, Spokesperson: Benny Wenda and three executive members are Leoni Tangama, Rex Rumaikek and Yakob Rumbiak. Council Committee automatically is replaced by top leaders of three main political party were Edison Waromi, Bucthar Tabuni and Richard Yoweni.

In the context of national leadership it is very sensitive amongst the Papuan group, it is not a hierarchical leader. Mote said *I am not a key national leader but I am coordinating leader same level with you all leaders*. A wise decission made in time will tell us to elects core leaders or national leaders. However, this leadership structure were agreed by all party and it was successful under government of Vanuatu endorsement. Now entry to strong new leadership era of movement then waiting for judgement by regional leaders for legal recognition that West Papua unity is complate under strong leadership structure. ULMWP is the only legitimated umbrella independence group by MSG then this regional government recognition on ULMWP was absolutely rewarding and extraordinary diplomacy success, next step is looking for PIF and UN.

III. ECONOMIC GLOBALISATION FORCE

The economic globalization notion and its impact must be uttermost lesson to comprehend by native West Papuans. In general draw various views and it could be classified into three level of the knowledge understanding (nothing, poor, enough), most of people believe that technological and industrial development is more helpful in progressing people's lifestyle, civilian will be luxury, well advantaged and the poor will be eradicated from poverty suffer. Their normative conception by new development of manufactures, textiles, automotive and exploring natural resources is always expected to have a good will that can lead to significant development in local economic growth and social welfare, more justice and equitable. Many local leaders already have influenced by globalists or competitors, capitalists, colonialists and imperialists but only few local leaders persistently uphold their natural talent in confronting the globalization disparity. West Papuan's dogma simply said "when the open new location; mountain, soil or land the natural spirit will be killed without permission to the landowner" and without cultural ceremony and those local leaders have to agree not by representation even naturally they have the ability to forecast the future consequences.

Free market and trade policy is a new globalisation economy model. What impact it has on local economy and social security in the third world nations and non-self-governing territory? Some economist indicated the global free market and trade is fundamental factor in doing globalisation work but failed to develop a global justice development for its economic growth into developing countries. This free global market and trade system considered by the colonialist ruling as the new economy order, the advantaged nations take pretty and million ways to re-colonise their former colonised nation by another form of economic power. Indonesia is good example, their master colonizer the Netherlands allows investment and trade in the region.

In the few globalisation books, all authors provide a very critical advice that independence sovereignty struggle should not be imposed by global economic regime, industrialised nations need to more humanistic approach not biased by self-ruled economic system. It is not simply to impose a global economic analysis opinion abolishes the word of colonialism. Modern economists like Adam Smith and Joseph S cleverly explain economic development theories, in their thoughts; free market and free trade can create opportunity in promoting the comparative advantage for growth. This idea is acceptable within capitalist society not to marginalised society groups. Comparative advantage consists of capital resources such as *Manpower, Machine, Method, Natural Resources* etc. Rich wealthy regions could get greater space to promote their comparative growth. West Papua's comparative advantage will not help the economic growth until free from foreign domination in the land. Indonesia and foreign party are dominant and ruling party in economic and business sector such as the *UNDP stated income from Papua's natural resource has not been invested sufficiently in service for the people.* It is not enough to provide a good public service alone or social security guarantee but more serious disparity is lack of opportunity for native population participation in economic business sector at all (small, medium and large). High flow for MNCs present equally economic marginalisation widespread into West Papuan community while the central government of Indonesia receiving a multiple incomes from tax, dividend and royalty payment.

West Papuan became the true victim of economic marginalisation within new global economy order, the global economy policies is not useful. The wealthy distribution from developed nations to poor nations, foreign or western investment, transfer technology and infrastructure, tax and employment are all of global plan are not part of West Papuan demands today because most of population depends on their sub-system economic lifestyle; hunting and farming and most paramount seeking for independence. So investment and infrastructure development can contribute negative risks for their survival and long life. West Papuan strongly condemns on a massive destruction of their natural healthy lifestyle, ancestral spirit, secret places and belief system for the past, now and in the future.

West Papua and Papua provinces have been categorized into four special economic zones in one of the Asian country who is the member of G20 which is Indonesia. According to Indonesian new investment plan, wanders to attract more foreign investment through special economic zone policy because of foreign investment benefit always fluctuated from the years 2013 counted $ 2.41 billion less than to 2014 was $1.41 billion. Therefore, Jakarta sets up new four Papuan economic zones in six potential sectors are mining, agriculture, food industry, storage, telecommunications and energy. Despite that BKPM has announced only four regions, they are Sorong for maritime and processing industry development, Merauke with Agriculture and farm industry, Raja Ampat for Tourism Industry, Teluk Bintuni for smelter and petro chemical industry, however, Indonesia will add more even all the region to be economically strategic regions because one of principal requirement of the government is the investor availability and ready to invest whole region.

Global economy forum of the G20 summit held in Brisbane 2014 confronted by over hundreds of protestors groups worldwide were gathered and standing on the street protest against the G20 leaders. The WPLM and IFWP has collaboratively addressed their plea directly to G20 leaders who have their own investment in West Papua such as Indonesia, Australia, US, UK, Japan, China, Canada and South Africa. In WPLM and IFWP's flayer sheet points out four key aspirations; *Firstly Stop global economic interest and MNCs activities; Secondly No misrepresentation on MOU investment and trade; Thirdly Pay international obligation on environmental protection, destruction and species extinction; Fourthly Given our democratic rights and rights to self-determination*. In the final G20 Leaders Communiqué they have produced many aspects but the only point in relevance to the aspiration by protestor groups namely G20 leaders agreed to tackle geopolitics as key challenger in global economy development and maintain social security in their global economy plan, more private sector engagement in infrastructures building and investment while maintain world obligation for environmental protection. In this geopolitics resolution, two approaches will take place, firstly peaceful ways of approaching all political parties, and radical ways is only interested party without other groups. It is a very likely challenge to

West Papua in where all natural resource under military control, and investment, monetary and fiscal fully control by Jakarta even with special autonomy plus law.

Husband (Amatus)_Wife (Bernarda) Protested during G20 Summit in Brisbane, Australia 2014

This picture was taken by ABC radio when Husband-Wife protested during four days of the G20 leaders meeting in Queensland 2014. One of West Papuan Activist, Rony Kareni also collaborated with others groups to protest Indonesian government. He said on the media that Jokowi do not forget West Papua's suffering and rights to self-determination and do not concern on your economic benefit from our rich land of West Papua. Husband-Wife had stipulated over thousands of pamphlet explain the reality of global economy interest undermine West Papua's rights. Their pamphlet talked about hopeless and miserable words; *during our life in foreign domination we have No democracy, No speech, No talk, No discuss, No choice, No dialogue,*

No referendum, No representatives, No signature, No agreement, No negotiation, No Freedom, No Rights, No Justice. No Peace and No Life. Our paradise and rich land stolen, our natural resources stolen, our leaders killed, our native religion extinct, our ancestral spirit dead. We lost everything on our paradise land. West Papua can be part of G20 after regain independence or became independent state nation for mutual global economic benefit for all the people and country.

Chapter IV

COPING
FUTURE DEVELOPMENT STRATEGIES

I. MOBILISE GLOBAL ASSISTANCE

After gaining regional recognition which was observer status at MSG, it will be faced with a critical phase internally and externally to drive up in terms of state nation forming vice versa seeking state nation recognition through international legal procedure. Independence struggle entry into more serious phase then needs to mobilise what the external and internal forces. External force development classify five most crucial aspect to discuss includes of Mobilise International Movement, Proper Diplomacy and Lobby Strategy, Effective Unity Coordination, Building Trust, and National Unity Education.

a. Mobilise International Movement

Need a wider network and link gain a greater support both physically and non-physically assistance. Physical support is non-diplomatic tools such as military aid and financial aid from the international community. Non-physical aid is ritual celebration and other diplomatic efforts. These efforts are asked to wider world society participation. What the world community groups are state members, religion groups, and UN entities, MNCs, TNM and NGOs/CSOs.

b. Proper Diplomacy and Lobby Strategies

The knowledge and skill development for young diplomats, training support and provide the opportunity to act themselves as their placement in where ULMWP office is based all around the world. Lobby strategies should begin from the regional block to international forum level. A critical strategy is to be backward from the historical perspective and forward perspective for future diplomacy and lobby. The 30 absent and other non-vote states for the Act of Free Choice, 24 committee members, PIF, Non-Alien Movement, African Union and European Union.

c. Effective Unity Coordination

It is strategically vital how to mobilise all resources, capacity and sharing responsibility. Many country and many groups is not a problem, the use of their political organisation but these groups must make registration and coordination under Umbrella Group of United Liberation Movement for West Papua. Currently it has seen a very effective coordination work by sharing diplomacy responsibility for membership bid at MSG. Octovianus Mote PNG and Fiji who assisted by Rosa in Fiji, Jakob Rumbiak in Solomon Island, Benny Wenda in Papua New Guinea but deported by emigration taken place Octovianus Mote, Leoni Tanggama and Rex Rumakiek in Kanaky and Amatus Douw for MSG secretariat and Vanuatu. Effective unity coordination again has seen a good cooperation inside West Papua under ULMWP, awareness and education West Papuan people about ULMWP and rising money for Vanuatu Cyclone Pam under this umbrella.

d. Building Trust

Building trust between and in both Papuan diplomat and foreign supporters is a good method to consolidate a stronger collective action. The rule of game for the liberation movement work is to be respected by any means. It might be half of world population who knows the West Papuan case distrust, by losing their trust means losing network and supporters worldwide. Foreign citizen aspiration can be good impact and attract wider support; they can call their own government attention in any particular country worldwide. Trust building is more vital in some technical and practical aspects for this liberation movement move; it also shapes the intelligence related work such as supply information and many other things.

Pro Indonesia of Papuan group must stop their betrayal activity by any means. Peaceful consolidation and cooperation is the best advice how to bring them back into right track, more encouragement of how important for WPNLM if they have enough courage to joint in independence movement. It can takes by peace talks to this groups internally that mediated by third party is considered to one of top agenda. Second ways is only by warning execution and lastly dead execution or dead row why no, they are definite betrayers and killers for future generation; they are real enemy like Indonesia. The case is many foreign government leader and diplomats asked why some of West Papuan are supporting Indonesia integrity and sovereignty, in order to answer that critical question, it not only takes special consideration by foreign government or world community the only way it can do is those West Papuan betrayer or traders must punish them under the national revolution law, if necessary take serious sanction for final execution.

e. National Unity Education

National unity education is a basic course for all political faction to clean up their misunderstandings and misconception before driving political revolution. Various political factions are good when they only promote the targeted political goal of independence. National unity education has been taken under the newly formed umbrella groups of ULMWP and it was a wining moment for its national unity proposes. Awareness and publication is a must for sustainable agenda to maintain this strong unity for future. Not to form new organisation, do not judge who the best within internal parties of ULMWP.

Internal Force Development is National Unity and Building Trust. National Unity is the key on how West Papuan pro and contra groups inside builds a one common understanding as one family within foreign rule. Ideology and notion differences need to be encouraged to Pro Indonesian groups. Indonesia has already brain washed some Papuan nationalist, especially officials of both the West Papua province and Papua province but they are not Indonesian, their heart is broken and want to separate. A good example two Papuan governors (Lukas Enembe and Abraham Ataruri) who invited by Jakarta to present at the MSG meeting in Solomon Islands but they missed. The both governors were recognised ULMWP as representative body of West Papuan at all then MSG leaders and world leaders understood what true West Papuan independence is and how they are now united to form a sovereignty state nation.

Internal Force development became challenging with regards to domestic political affairs, off course Indonesia is fuming and pro-active to complain about it. Indonesia has banned the national unity and identity project was conducted by ULMWP on March 2015, by entitled *seeking a true identity by West Papua returning to the MSG family*. INP has repressively stopped them when organising committee of ULMWP invited all level of element, provincial worker for forming common concept about nationalism and identity forum discussion. INP more oppressive action has shown, shot dead of a West Papuan and three of them wounded during rising fund for Vanuatu under ULMWP coordination. Foreign government and global civil society groups are watching, public critics on this repression from everywhere, therefore by such Indonesian security organs action will have duel impact, namely people are getting traumatised, getting scary and more wider attention. However, Team Work of ULMWP has been educating all unsure of society in West Papua, many migrant were part of the awareness plan successfully like over 2000 signatures to support ULMWP. National unity was awakening both in home and exile.

Education and awareness into targeted group publicly. Identify West Papuan betrayer and intelligent working within colonial government of Indonesia at all society groups from religious, customary, women, student and youth. Sustainable national unity can be achieved by public education and publishing a little booklet is good lesson book. Team work of ULMWP had written a book about ULMWP must be given free to those targeted people so that they can know what their vision about their future determination and their future generation as Melanesian Papuans though is like.

II. ADVOCACY TO WORLD BODY
II.1. THE 24 COMMITTEE OF THE UN

New world rule twisted for all groups participation in world politics whether state and non-state including legitimated groups of NLM or not at common in the process towards state nations building process. NSGT at UN luckily is an active member in global politics players. Previously they were waiting longer time people under the colonial repression were not on the 24 committee, they have struggled to get decolonisation status now they are enjoying on the committee board. UN 24 committee inspiring other non-legitimated groups of NLM and NSGT not on the list to be able access such West Papua to express their political aspiration, the decolonisation is unfinished political business in the world politics, the term of eradication of colonialism will not finish until all colonial territories which are both on the list and not on the list get their inalienable rights and independence.

With decolonisation status has more balances of power amongst triple parties namely Indonesia, UN and West Papua to work it out in accomplishment of the targeted program in politics, economic, democracy and security. As world knows the complexity problem in West Papua holistically must not be addressed under current global structure and colonial regime, it does not mean these programs and plan are ruled by the administering government, West Papuan will have shared power and responsibility in implementation to tackle these matters.

West Papua on the 24 Committee, given below is an idea that can contribute what the future major challenges for gaining independence state. Before it goes through the essential criteria is development capacity in the process of nation state building.

II.2. INTERNATIONAL COURT OF JUSTICE

Why the course must ask a legal judgement through world court system and what procedures and strategies can be useful to bring this court case and what are the parties necessary to invite them to clarify past injustice and misleading their world obligation as they are state party. State party are US, Indonesia, Netherlands and UN. International pacific settlement on world disputes are very clear point for everybody in accordance the protocols whether state party or non-state party. For the territorial matter, sovereignty and human crime that those are not finished yet bring those perpetrators and injustice in the world justice table. Non-legitimated and legitimated National Liberation Movement party can also be qualified to be core party in the world justice procedure, there is no prohibited rule to stop by any other party.

Legal Opinion Inquiry is the international protocol for everyone whoever state actor or non-state actor has rights and free to submit an inquiry whatever course if all the legal conditions are fulfilled there is no matter win or lose. Lose and win is the final outcome for constructed parties or conflict parties who obligate to receipt in the end. In order to maintain a justice there is no one higher than justice law only creator for the God Believers, principally, ICJ holding a highest authority not state members even five veto rights states or UN itself. It ensures all the legal procedure before move up, do not need to hesitate or scary with the colonialist power and their power if the party who is targeted to bring to the court is one of veto rights states like USA. West Papuan people has to stand on their justice and freedom, there is no choice to find other legal opinion by other ways or system.

ICJ is an international legal body at the UN system that consists of 15 member in which five permanent vote rights states and other 10 non-veto rights states. UN and a permanent state member were involved in the political annexation according to historical fact, world judicial system cannot be discriminate by any power or manipulate by any membership power. The only issue will be there is the procedure barrier. This mitigation needs to be a serious work before they qualify the legal procedure not fear from US as leading world power and controlling UN system. To get a clear insight learn from the other similar cases from other countries for example Palestine and Tibet then, why West Papua Territory is cannot go to legal trial?

African, Pacific, Caribbean and American Latin nations were stressed to look for more formal justice ways to review the political status of the West Papua. Solomon Islands and Vanuatu, Ghana and Senegal ready to challenging the AFC to ICJ according to official website of Solomon Islands government. Solomon Island's Special envoy for West Papua has been travelling to those countries to convince and make sure of their support and willingness for the legal process. Guayana also was interested in the court case; international human rights lawyer from Guayana is cofounder for ILWP now coming more lawyers from Australia and UK more focal one. Melanesian regional body needs to consider this court case, that is gone be work when MSG authority support it in name of regional government. Mobilisation states support, legal entity and global community stand behind West Papua are very vital.

II.3. International Criminal Court

Indonesian state criminality needs to be brought before the ICC. It should not wait after independence, it will help out to open all the cases towards a final dream of independence, Indonesian violations must be judged in the eyes of the world community, West Papuans cannot give them amnesty or clemency. Then what are the criminal realities that need to be prepared as central instrument condition to defend their claim for justice. What other interested parties have to invite whether state party or non-state party, they can be MNCs even foreign religion were involved in denial for human rights principals. The all party been involved in genocide the life of West Papuan are Indonesia Freeport McMoran or might be foreign religion. West Papuan has no choice in defending those religions that fought against native religion and believers in the early. Hundreds of thousands of people were dead in many places, it is against humanity and fundamental sovereignty rights of native West Papuan to freely and peacefully maintain the original belief system.

Blatant human rights tension just recently brings to the attention by regional government for sanction to judge these violator parties from the all interested parties in regards to natural resource exploitation. PIF Secretariat on sub regional committee has passed a recommendation on giving a sanction to private and public corporation who involved in human rights violation. The worldwide NGOs groups and West Papuan has now become more confident if regional leaders set out in their regional plan for implementation for their leaders' summit in Port Moresby 2015. Nevertheless, there are some barriers that have seen before the regional decision taking place because few of pacific countries owned company also took part in the violation such as the Rio Tinto and other mining from Australia. Human rights sanction is not only killing people, marginalisation but also environmental degradation and killing of native species. It is very positive to maintain social security principles on the negative exercises by the corporation who victimise native people or landowners to take more serious step at least bring to the world criminal court. West Papuan people has different faith with other former colonial people like Timor Leste, they give clemency to Indonesia criminal state never brought to ICC for justice. It is good idea to think that how West Papua and Timor Leste would like to open Indonesian state criminalities at the world court table.

III. NATIONALISM DEVELOPMENT

National identity development is very complex and unique. What the core components of national identity basically refers to is ethnicity, culture, religion and social structures, it is questionable whether it still survives or not. West Papua consists of 312 local ethnicities within seven customary division regions includes of MEPAGO, LAPAGO, SAIRERI, MANTA, ANHIM AH, DOMBERAI and BOMBERAI. There is no other foundation upon the Melanesian territory from the Dutch time to Indonesian rule over three century in the true fact and this reality is acceptable that it will be core barrier in Papuan nationalism construction in the future.

Internationally, the West Papuan society groups, their true political identity of this group as part of decolonised people or Non-self governing territory. In international used this groups is not indigenous people but there is minority decolonised people or LWN. Personally disagree to put the groups into other groups or indegenous, why the writer would like to explain more deeply:

1. West Papuan is not part of World Indegenous people group and trust territory.

2. Political and legal status of Papua is not indigenous classification, they still have to finish this status quo for decolonisation.

3. Not in the name of West Papua state colonising but in the

name of Unitary State of Republic of Indonesia, then West Papuan political status diffrent to other indigenous nations such Aborigin, Indian in America, Maori in New Zealand.

4. Presiden of World Indigenous Forum clearly said that the West Papua case is not Indigenous matter but they are colonised people, the better place to put is the decolonisation committee. Even few West Papuan under the West Papua Liberation Organisation dealing to indigenous matter, the term used in the international politics would be different favourite, not for independence.

III.1. STATE NATION FORMATION

Native norms and ethics in West Papua should to be saved for nation's state building. It is very much connected about how they uphold normative natural law that can give a good impact for today's independence struggle movement for state nation building. Learn from theoretical perspective what the important on the nationalism and anthropological insight. It has been absolutely explained in more clearly the traditional society consists of a groups of people maintain their lifestyle, religion and cultures structurally ruled up into bureaucratic system. The formation of state nation theory is also very much derived by radical approaches such as religion, cultural norms and ethics as the fundamental factor for instance Islamic states and Christian states in the real world today. In political spectrum they have advised to understand better what the key inspiration force in independence movement, the most fundamental aspect for surviving on this oldest belief system (religion, culture and land). The first political manifesto and its constitutional stated as nation upholding the natural law of tolerance and freedom of religion for each country around the world. Here history is educating us that the morning star was designed to native norms from Biak Islands "Koreri Movement (original religion of Biak people). Morning star is lighter and director for people and other creates in the land according to norm, it is a heritage duty to maintain it up by every generation because it is symbol of lighter given by GOD or Manseren.

From the 312 tribes, their own believe system. Just in a small number those native religions that survived until now are Bunani and Koreri, this is totally dissimilar to other modern religion. Writer does strongly believe that to build up the sense of belonging is what our own religion will help for younger in the future.

Seeking an original national identity of Papua is crucially vital to be part of pacific cultural community kinship program from the Melanesian linkage. In terms of building Melanesian national identity, MSG already welcomed ULMWP to Observer Status but only representing Melanesian Papuan in exile not at whole population, this recognition come from the MSG leaders only. Does West Papuan build up a Christian state in West Papua without barrier if all Christian nations given independence and most of Melanesian nations are majority Christian? While Indonesia is an associated member state at MSG Indonesia might not allow even build up a Muslim state in West Papua. Now coming to question that how native religion norms and ethics contribute in our state nation formation process.

Could we be able to form our native one "Bunani and Koreri state or others" in West Papua why not?

West Papuan people cannot say it is too late or it is a very odd idea. West Papuan has already learned from the past colonial experience by different dominant states and cultures. A historical experience has strongly proven that West Papuan is in the slow genocide motion at all aspect not only human being in the Melanesian territory. Many academics, UN experts, government diplomat, international community incredibility have a big aware that from year of 2040 will be leads to extinction; it means no life and dead for future generation. From the Dutch until to Indonesian hegemony, their domination is part world's popular culture like their lifestyle, culture and religion. Dutch was introduced to establish state nations as Christianity state nation but it has failed and empty promise to put place into realisation meanwhile within Indonesia with Muslim domination also failed to convince West Papuan to be independent state nation as well. All the brilliant argumentation here will introduce series of social realities for nearly two century under foreign domination that resulted genocide in different dimension of life, the richest world number first Islands depleted and the holy virgin land destructed, holy man/women were killed, the spiritual strength broke, powerful and charismatic leaders killed until independence leader dead. Foreign religion faith is unable to bring a good life and salvation for native Melanesian of West Papuan.

It is a new paradigm for the state nation's formation if West Papuans are willing to build up a native religion state system such as Bunani and Koreri. West Papua Territory will be the first nation all around world in the 21st Century. People need to know that it is not ethno nation state wants to be like western theoretical rhetoric, example of native Bunani system born from the beginning age then native religion could be articulate *Alpha and Omega*. People must recognise themselves that they are the first people born in their first native system before the foreign system came over to destroy your native one. From the seven customary regions that have similar system they have got before, sadly some of them are extinct already; only few of them are still active in secret places by secret ways. They have democracy system, organisational and leadership structure, meaningful and sacral symbol, cabinet and covenant, their Bunani official language unlike the Mee language truly, not only Bunani but also the other native religion too. West Papuan is very rich and unique traditional system from the religion structure to social community configuration, from the arts to culture, all universality in one nation and one society, one land which is based on the national motto that is *one people one soul*.

III. 2. SPIRITUAL DEVELOPMENT

Entire region in West Papua have their native religion such as Koreri from Saireri and Bunani from Mee Pago and other religions from the five customary regions. One of the academy researcher said *in the context of West Papua this will be extremely difficult due to the penetration of the popular western culture through television and migrant workers the Muslim way of life within Indonesia, and the Christianisation of Papuan population by American and Australian missionaries.* Infiltration of the world's popular cultures into minority traditional society case study of West Papuan community is not new social phenomenon; it is really human calamity and rooting in the traditional society system. It will be an explicit impediment and utopia in terms of reconstruction context even rebuilding for the Papuan native belief system one in the future. Most substantially re-establishes the entire ethnical spiritual strength, the diversity those are native religion, gathering natural spirit, discover the oldest norms and ethics of belief system. Why is it important to do it this way and how to vitalise in this contemporary time need to be deeper explanation of this study for conceptual undertsanding. But practical explanation is very easy by telling history and dicussion as informal education from the family like telling about the real story and or tales around it.

Papuan original spritual power led to extinction since the European Missionaries were founded in the entire land of Melanesian. The using of the Jesus Christ names via European belief system impacted the true long native God name of Papuan was forced away. On 5 February 1855, Otto and Geissler, Germanian Missioaris first landed at Mansinam Island, they declared that in the name of Jesus Christ or Lord we feed this land. It means that the ideology of christianity and western spritual power were establised now rooting at the underground. 5 February many people recognised a peace day, but writer provides opposition on that opinion, this day is the first day in destroying West Papuan native religion especially Koreri from Mansinam Island because in reality a lot of figthing was involved, this secret religion war did not find out but also telling history by secretly. Indeed, foreign missionaries or priest can use some wise wording in term of changing the melanesian way of thinking on their original belief system. Actually, God gives a good wisdom for West Papuan to see what the motif of outsider influence, everybody is truly not perspect only God despite somebody can serve sermon in wise words or the word of God does not mean that is right and good for you. West Papuan are people with high moral character in tolerance that why foreign misionaries welcomed in their home country. Interfaith tolerancy is most meaningful aspect to respect one another, if country owner gives you tolerance to run your religious service how to you behave, you must pay back your good tolerance to the landower in relation to not geoparadise their own native religion.

Many people strongly argue about foreign religious teaching and its misintrepretation. Most of traditional society from the third world nations believe that it has found the city of God only in the way of western belief or through Jesus Christ; *I am the way of God, without me no one goes to Heaven and God,* it is true for Western Christianity flowers because their native religion. However, it is wrong in the eye of the other religions pespective, this is what the christianity had imposed Papuan native belief system while today's Muslim teaching is more radical. Muslim and Christian education seemly be irrational theacing because of the religion is not one, nation is not one, culture is not one. God as Creator is ONE for all religions and nations in the univers but the ways to go to God absolutely has many direction according to each religious faith in the earth's planet. In common Gospel values said do not steel and do not kill. It explicitly explains that the way to go and maintain a good relationship with God you must to go the way that God gives before you. The first or original religion given to you by God is the awsome one to follow him.

Majority of Papuan people lost their native religion because of some fundamental factors:

1. Negative prejudice and sterotpyes through modern religion values influence in their teaching called the native Papuan religion classifed as animism and dynimism or belief to godess so not will go to heaven in the end of life.
2. All spritual materials burnt out and taken away out in the name of Western Lord.
3. Islamic influence is more rooted in every single of the natural spiritual power by two ways collecting and killed the Papuan natural spirit power including gather powerful spiritual materials.
4. Buddist and Hinduism also took part by their religion teaching and worship and took away all Papuan spritual power and threw them out.

NATIVE RELIGION:

It is substantial to know for the West Papuan people in the 21st century that how and where their ancestor built holy relationship with God and its creator in the past. Good suggestion is to explore the characteristics of local Papuan religion, its diversity is to clean up stereotype ideas in Papuan mind that there is no God in West Papua, No Religion, No Bless come from God Creator, Believe to Animism and dynamism not God and others led crisis their natural pure identity of belief system. To throw out entire colonialists's misinterpretation like negative images of these Melanesian heritages possession, valuable materials and other that those is hell tools if Papuan hold it you will die and you will not go to heaven. The critical question is who the creator of those things, God or anyone else? This is one of the colonisation system politely used by foreigners to occupy in moral and spiritual ways.

Many western writers critically argue that Western Christianity doctrines undermine other native religions across the world. The idea of other native religion was born after Christianity and Muslim, therefore, indoctrination or generalisation from the both popular religion is absolutely a mistake. Writer strongly disagrees that Eben Kirksey has expressed Bunani was originally from Sakeus Pakage teaching after he gained the Christian theology degree from Australia. Sakeus Pakage was a leader of Kingmi Church or Utouwege movement. Utouwege and Bunani are fundamentally two different faiths. Bunani is the only native religion, but Utouwege is the movement by Protestants followers they belong to Christianity. Writer was born and grew up in both Bunani and Utouwege back ground family, hence, very well understood about their faith distinction and in this book writer would like to make a clear picture, however, the both teaching about the true and truth generally. It is very bad and sad history that's why Sakeus Pakage was killed in Dutch prison because his teaching on family unity or togetherness in the faith of Christianity.

To rebuild up true native identity is a very hard job in the era of globalisation and modernisation, people minds and heart might say it is too odd, invaluable, ancient or old or primitive lifestyle. Many theorists agree this critical opinion because the world is already spread out by the popular cultural and religion of the European traditional belief system namely Christianity, Middle East native religion of Muslim, Asian with Buddhist, Hinduism and Khonghucu. In West Papua, there are numerous native Melanesian religion actively survive around the land of Papua from the coastal areas up to highland or mountain, their native one believes God to be as creator of its religion. Unfortunately, originality and neutrality for the native belief system has almost sunk in the foreign religion hegemony constrain, it is a real utopia. All the tribal people go to their first religion before colonialism begun, at present the revolutionary time should have enough time to be one of the primary agenda of nationalism and identity building program. Writer strongly advices that it can use political or independence revolution momentum for the original religion revolution needs to be a core program in the independence struggle period. A good suggestion from the Papuan native believer is that freedom fighters must pray in their native religious way for their independence plea because God has given the independence definitely will come through in that direction.

NATURAL SPIRIT

Building a good connection with all the natural spirits is not bad, neither does it sound odd, despite that we live in this secular planet, nor is it very positive in terms of asking their blessings and strength. Call back the million natural Papuan spirits stolen by outsider; to keep in life all killed those good natural spirits by modern killer. The modern killer consists of foreign religion, teaching on realistic, corporation, and colonialist states. Natural spirit still survived even in the 20th century. People cannot articulate the natural spirit that has already gone because it can reside inside of the humankind; humans and the natural spirit do have instructions via three vital components of humans that are soul, mind and body as the natural spirit is moveable.

From the many planets, what we have got in our world, our planet Earth is the only one point of the universe, the Astronomers might know how big and what it's content but not the whole. Spiritually, everyone believes in their own way, which is totally different to scientific approach though and from many religious views also natural spirit just outside which connects the universe and human being. Even today is global era, everything with digital world, from the bottom people can recognise that natural spirits never go away from human life. For a scientist world's view might be different, theory of everything from natural science perspective explains about gravitation and cosmic view that the theory also never trusts God, nevertheless theorists trust the natural spirit. Religious and realist views' differences are vital to find the ways how to integrate into one common conceptual understanding it brings a good intension between them. For West Papuan native religious views that natural spirit and holy spirit is one of the forms of spirit, it is not about bad and good spirit. Holy Spirit is mostly the Christian community's belief, but both natural spirit and holy spirit comes from God, the Creator. There is nothing about bad or negative connotation; only the humans have wrong conception as they believe that they are natural spirit from the universe and holy from the God.

BIBLIOGRAPHY

- Ana, K et al 2012, *Conflict and identification of the Least Developed Countries: theoretical and statistical considerations*, Economic and Social Affairs, Paper No, 13, February, 2012.

- APEC Indonesia 2013, Bali Declaration *Resilient Asia-Pacific, Engine of Global Growth,* THE 21ST APEC ECONOMIC LEADERS' DECLARATION, 8 October 2013, Bali Indonesia

- Asia Pacific Economy Cooperation, APEC INDONESIA 2013, 8 October 2013, Bali.

- Bland B & Donnan S, high quality global journalism requires investment, 26 March, 2014 Jakarta & London. (http://www.ft.com/cms/s/0/3755c)

- Denney, L 2012, *Security: the missing bottom of the millennium development goals; prospects for inclusion in the post-MDG development framework*, Overseas Development Institute Paper.

- Elmslie J, 2010, West Papua Demographic Transition and the 2010 Indonesia Census: " Slow Motion Genocide" or Not (http://sydney.edu.au/arts/peace_conflict/docs/working_papers/West_Papuan_D)

- Gasser, P1979, *Internationalised non-international armed conflicts: case studies of Afghanistan, Kampuchea and Lebanon.* (http://www.wcl.american.edu/journal/lawrev/33/gasser.pdf)

- Haluk M 2013, hidup atau mati;*hilangnya harapan hidup dan hak asasi manusia di Papua*, Deyai, Indonesia.

- Hauss, C2001, *international conflict resolution; international relations for the 21st century, CONTINUM*, London and New York.

- Khan, I , Gul 2012, *Afghanistan: Human Cost of Armed Conflict since the Soviet Invasion*, PERCEPTIONS, Volume XVII, No 4,pp.209-224,

- Kirksey, E 2012 freedom in an entangled world, online source (http://ebenkirksey.blogspot.com.au/),

- Lehtinen, T 2001, the *forgotten war in the Congo*, Congo.

- Lnnie D, 2011, Technical Report, West Wist Mining Limited Derewo River Gold Projects, Papua, Indonesia, CSG Global Resources Industry Consultant, WA, Australia

- Macleod, J 2003, Standing Up for West Papua: *How Australia profits from an illegal and brutal occupation and what you can do about it.*

- Mayanja, R 2010, *armed conflict and women: 10 years of Security Council resolution 1325 (UN).*

- Muhammad, C 2006, The *Environmental Impacts of Freeport-Rio Tinto's Copper and Gold Mining Operation in Papua,* WALHI - Indonesian Forum for Environment, Jakarta.

- Murray S & Cullen A 2011, *the globalization of world politics: case studies from Australia-pacific*, 5th edn, Oxford University press, New York.

- Ondawame, O 2010, *one people, one soul; West Papuan nationalism and the organisasi papua merdeka*, Crawford House Publishing, Adelaide, Australia.

- Owens, et al 2011, *the globalization of the world politics; an introduction to international relation*, 5th edn, OXFORD UNIVERSITY PRESS, New York.

- PACIFIC ISLANDS FORUM SECRETARIAT, Forum Communiqué, Thirty-Seventh Pacific Islands Forum, 24–25 OCTOBER 2006, Nadi, Fiji

- PACIFIC ISLANDS FORUM SECRETARIAT, Forum Communiqué, Thirty-Third Pacific Islands Forum, 15–22 August 2002, Nadi, Fiji

- Pacific Islands Forum Secretariat, 46 th Pacific Islands Forum Communique, 7-11 September, Port Moresby, PNG.

- Power, R 2008, *law of armed conflict (LOAC)*, http://usmilitary. about.com/cs/wars/a/loac.htm.

- Quaker Peace & Legislation Committee, QPLC DISCUSSION PAPER: INDONESIA and AUSTRALIA, Canberra 2014

- Regional Development Planning Agency Papua province, Harmonisation of development artners; support for human development in Papua Province, 6th Edition, 2009

- Rolings, L 2010, the west Papua dilemma, university of Wollongong thesis collection, University Wollongong research online

- Saltford, F John, 2000, *'UNTEA and UNRWI: United Nations Involvement in West New Guinea during the 1960's', a Thesis submitted for the Degree of Doctor of Philosophy, University of Hull.*

- Sakhong, L 2012, *the Dynamics of Sixty Years of Ethnic Armed Conflict in Burma*, Analysis Paper No.1 pp1-15.

- Sharp N & Kaisiepo Wongor M, 1991, The morning star in Papua Barat, Arena publication, Victoria Australia,

- Slovakia, B 2001, *the impact of armed conflict on women and Girls A consultative meeting on mainstreaming gender in areas of conflict and reconstruction*, United Nations Population Fund Report, 2001

- Smith, A 2011, *the hidden crisis: Armed conflict and education*, Education for All Global Monitoring Report 2011, UNESCO.

- Sttot, A 2011, Would An Independent West Papua Be A Failing State, The Asia-Pacific Journal Vol 9, Issue 37 No 1, September 12, 2011.

- Team Kerja Jaringan Damai Papua, 2010, *Jakarta_Papua Dialogue*, Jayapura, West Papua.(http://jdp-dialog.org/profil/ koordinator-jdp)

- Tebay, N 2006, *interfaith endeavour in West Papua*, Otmar, MISSIO, German.

- Tim Sosialisasi Aceh Damai, 2005. Memorandum of Understanding between the Government of the Republic of Indonesia and the Free Aceh Movement. BRR, Banda Aceh.

- UNAMA, 2013, Afghanistan *Annual Report 2012 protection of civilians in armed conflict*, February 2013, Kabul, Afghanistan.

- United Nations Development Program 2011/2012 Annual Report, *Empowered Life, resilient Nations,* UNDP Indonesia, Jakarta

- US Energy Information Administration, 5 march 2014

www.ingramcontent.com/pod-product-compliance
Lightning Source LLC
Chambersburg PA
CBHW072119020426
42334CB00018B/1645